The European Tribe

Caryl Phillips was born in St Kitts West Indies, in 1958. Brought up in England, he has written for television, radio, theatre and the screen. He is also the author of five novels, *The Final Passage*, *A State of Independence*, *Higher Ground*, *Cambridge* and *Crossing the River*. His awards include the Martin Luther King Jr. Memorial Prize and a Guggenheim Fellowship. He is writer-in-residence at Amherst College, Massachusetts.

Caryl Phillips

The European Tribe

First published 1987 by Farrar, Straus & Giroux, New York

First published in Great Britain in Picador 1993 by Pan Books Limited
a division of Pan Macmillan Publishers Limited
Cavaye Place London SW10 9PG
and Basingstoke

Associated companies throughout the world

ISBN 0 330 32989 8

Copyright © Caryl Phillips 1987, 1992

1 3 5 7 9 8 6 4 2

A CIP catalogue record for this book is available from
the British Library

Printed and bound in Great Britain by
Cox & Wyman Ltd, Reading, Berkshire

Europe: a continent extending from Asia to the Atlantic
        Ocean.
Tribe: a racial group (especially in a primitive or nomadic
        culture) living as a community under one or more
        chiefs.

Even if I did speak Irish I'd always be an outsider here,
wouldn't I? I may learn the password but the language of the
tribe will always elude me, won't it? The private core will
always be . . . hermetic, won't it?

Brian Friel, *Translations*, 1981

The English language
belongs to us. You are raking at dead fires,
a waste of time for somebody your age.
That subject people stuff is a cod's game,
infantile, like your peasant pilgrimage.

Seamus Heaney, 'Station Island', 1984

For Trevor, Malcolm and Tony

Contents

Foreword

It is almost ten years since I first thought of travelling across Europe and writing a book of essays about my experiences. I eventually undertook the journey in 1984, and three years later *The European Tribe* was published. Were I planning such a journey today, and spread before me was a map of Europe, I would be faced with a continent whose political boundaries and systems of government have altered radically. The problems of securing visas for visiting Eastern Europe, of paying in 'hard' currencies, of seeking in vain to obtain permission to travel to resticted areas, all are now somewhat alleviated. Similarly, in the west, travel between the countries of the Common Market is easier, as the twelve member nations inch their reluctant way towards some form of political federalism. However, what seem to me the most interesting aspects of a changing Europe are not so much the questions that relate to borders and the ever-mutable map, but those that address the more specific problems of tribalism and racism in the soul of Europe. A consideration of these problems underpins many of the essays in *The European Tribe,* and in the last ten years the rise of nationalistic fervor, which leads people to close ranks into groups—or tribes—has become *the* most urgent and seemingly intractable of the many difficulties that now face modern Europe.

That I had the temerity to regard Europe as tribal caused some eyebrows to be raised back then. However, a decade on, the facts seem to speak for themselves. The Soviet Union has fallen apart along national lines, with countries that were denied an identity under the red flag now reasserting themselves. Yugoslavia has shattered along historical stress lines. Czechoslovakia is about to be cleaved in half. The terrorist campaigns of the Basques in Spain and the Irish in Britain have not abated. The tribes of Europe are forever suspicious of each other. They nurse old hurts close to their chests, they are anxious to protect national identities, they continue to fracture along deep fissures that no amount of political goodwill seems able to heal. To my mind this appears unsurprising, for Europeans are simply responding to socio-economic pressure in much the same way as people in other parts of the world. However, the danger of rampant tribalism, whether it emerges as a result of asserting nationalism, in the east, or of combating federalism, in the west, is that in order to affirm who you are as a people you must also create a class of people who are not you. Who are different. Who are outsiders. Who can never be you. Who are less than you.

A significant increase in intolerance towards outsiders, be they immigrants, seasonal workers, political refugees, or nationals of a different skin colour or faith, has been the most disturbing feature of the last decade. A deeply ingrained institutionalized racism, which discriminates with particular virulence in the housing and job market, has always been a part of the European way of life. But unprovoked attacks and murder, although by no means a new phenomenon, have now become disturbingly common. A brief survey of some recent headlines in the *quality* British press reveals something of the range and depth of this malaise. "Racist Russians loathe the rise of Caucasian 'Blacks' " (*Observer*). "Neo-Nazis wring concessions from German opposition" (*The Times*). "Racism finds fertile ground in Hungary" (*Independent*). "Italy's latent racism wakes up on the back streets of Florence" (*Independent*). "Swedes turn to racist backlash" (*Guardian*). I could continue. The list is almost endless. What I found surprising when looking at these newpapers was the lack of reportage concerning British racism. It certainly exists, but perhaps I would have to go to France or Germany, and look in their newspapers, in order to read about what is happening in Britain.

Shortly after the publication of *The European Tribe* I decided to spend time living and writing in the Caribbean. I wanted to explore the other part of me. The part of me which felt 'not of Europe.' Since then I have lived and worked back in London, and in Stockholm. More recently, I have lived in the United Sates of America, a country in which I now spend more time than I do in Europe. The peripatetic nature of my life is probably more a response to my chosen profession as a writer than a statement of any terminal dissatisfaction with Europe. However, it would be disingenuous of me to pretend that there are not aspects of Europe that continue to both infuriate and disappoint me. These range from Europe becoming little more than a cultural outpost of North America, lapping up satellite television and Euro-Disney with glee, to the more disturbing development of 'ethnic cleansing' in Yugoslavia. The phrase itself is probably the most chilling euphemism for racially motivated murder since 'the final solution.'

I wrote *The European Tribe* while consumed with the anxieties of knowing that I was a member of the larger European tribe, a member who felt uncomfortable at being such, but who had no viable alternative. In the interim I have forged some alternatives, and I therefore look at Europe with perhaps a little more detachment. I continue to travel extensively across this land that I feel both of and not of, but I sometimes wonder if it is an exercise in futility to worry over the health of a continent which seems so sadly wedded to the ugly conceits of racism. Being neither a politician nor a social scientist, I have no suggestions as to how to combat tribalism, or the resultant racism that continues to stain Europe. There are, however, people of all colours and nationalities, of many religious and political persuasions, who are attempting to wrestle Europe's face around so that she might at least be forced to stare in the mirror. I wrote *The European Tribe* as a contribution to this process.

Caryl Phillips
London, 1992

Preface

This book is based on personal experience. It is not academic, nor does it have any pretensions to being able to survive the rigours of the sociologist's laboratory. It is a narrative in the form of a notebook in which I have jotted various thoughts about a Europe I feel both of and not of. Its impetus was provided by nearly a year's wandering from Europe's closest neighbour, Morocco, to her furthest flung capital, Moscow.

I am not the first writer of fiction to find that the tension between myself and my environment is so urgently felt that the fictional mould seems too delicate a vessel to hold it. However, in writing *The European Tribe* I soon discovered that rather than solving the question of what Europe means to me, the best I could hope for was that the experience might better define the parameters of my 'problem'.

During my travels I had reason to be grateful to Ian Gibson, Paul Webster, Jaco and Elizabeth Groot, Brian Friel, Stephen Castles, 'Peter' (in Poland), and Lindis Hallan. However, my greatest thanks go to my friend and editor, Frances Coady. Her patience, encouragement and commitment made this book possible.

Caryl Phillips
London, 1986

The European Tribe

Introduction

Had I been a bright student at school
I'd have learnt more and turned out to be a fool.

West Indian Calypsonian

You're a lost crowd, you educated Negroes, and you will only
find yourself in the roots of your own people. You can't choose
as your models the haughty-minded educated white youths of a
society living solid on its Imperial conquests.

Claude McKay, *Banjo*, 1929

Praise had bled my lines white of any more anger,
and snow had inducted me into white fellowships,
while Calibans howled down the barred streets of an empire
that began with Caedmon's raceless dew, and is ending
in the alleys of Brixton, burning like Turner's ships.

Derek Walcott, *Midsummer*, 1984

It was in the United States that I made the 'discovery' that it was possible for a black person to become, and sustain a career as, a writer. My ignorance probably came about as a result of my education and my own lack of a coherent sense of identity in 1970s Britain. In British schools I was never offered a text that had been penned by a black person, or that concerned the lives of black people. References to black people were confined to the playground. As a ten-year-old boy I remember my best friend telling me a 'joke'. 'There are', he said, 'a group of Pakis walking down the road singing "We shall overcome".' Obviously he had overheard his father, or one of his father's friends, in conversation. This was 1968, the year of Martin Luther King's assassination in Memphis, Tennessee, the year of Enoch Powell's 'rivers of blood' speech in Britain. These events were bound up in the 'joke', but all I can remember thinking was, 'I don't understand it.' I doubt that my friend Terry did either. But unlike him I could not laugh, and my silence marked the end of our friendship.

About three years later one of the most painful episodes of my childhood took place. This time it was inside a classroom. Mr Thompson, an English literature teacher, decided to demonstrate his knowledge of all things by explaining the origins of our surnames. So Greenberg was Jewish, Morley originally came from the small Yorkshire town of the same name, and McKenzie was a Scot. I felt a hot flush of embarrassment long before he turned towards my desk. 'Phillips,' he mused, 'you must be from Wales.' The whole class laughed, while I stared back at him stony-faced, knowing full well that I was not from Wales. The truth was I had no idea where I was from as I had been told that I was born in the Caribbean but came from England. I could not participate in a joke which made my identity a source of humour. Even those I considered my friends were laughing. If the teaching of English literature can feed a sense of identity then I, like many of my black contemporaries in Britain, was starving.

Looking back at Britain in the 1970s, I am now convinced that it must have been the worst decade since the Second World War to grow up in. It lacked the buoyant optimism of the 1950s, the liberal freedoms of the 1960s, and seems to have been characterized by tasteless and ephemeral fashions, third-rate music (a kind of post-Beatles despair), and a long and tedious preparation for the industrial decline and depression of the 1980s. As a first-generation migrant, I came to Britain at the portable age of twelve weeks; I grew up riddled with the cultural confusions of being black and British. I was at the older end of a generation who eventually found their communal voice in the Notting Hill riots of 1976.

This first expression of my generation's pent-up social anger came a little too late for me. I was already away at college with all my hang-ups intact. These were anxieties that grew from having been brought up in predominantly white working-class areas, which featured red disposal pipes, yellow-striped façades, and skylines broken up by twenty-four-storey blocks of flats. Two days after completion these estates are ghettos, there is dog shit all over the playgrounds so parents can't send the kids out to play, and within a month someone has been stabbed. In different times people have been known to burn such places down. My educational environment, in mainly white-dominated middle-class schools, only served to depress me further. However, the mid-1970s were also the years of Bob Marley and the Wailers, the film *Pressure*, and the emergence of black footballers and sportsmen into the mainstream of British cultural life. And I was gone, away at university.

Oxford is a divided city. Although there are many black people, most of whom are employed by the British Leyland car factory, the prevalent ethos is of 'town and gown'. I found that student life had its own momentum, and spurned much of what happened in the rest of the city. City dwellers held a similarly dismissive attitude towards the university, and collaborations between the two were few. This left the question of black people inside the university. There were some of us but not many, and the situation was made all the more frustrating by the collegiate system whereby students tended to mix with those in their own colleges rather than across the university spectrum.

At The Queen's College we had Patrick from Uganda, a brilliant mathematician who studied his books with one eye on the international pages of *The Times*. His doctoral studies were in danger of becoming his life's work, as a return to Uganda, which was still smarting from the Amin years of plunder and mismanagement, was not entirely appealing. He was unsure what to do, but all his family were there and it was home. There were also a couple of guys from Nigeria who I knew less well. Oseg was doing research into astrophysics and practically lived in the science department, while

3

Emmanual, the politics, philosophy and economics under-graduate, tended to live in the college bar. Like Patrick, their affair with Britain was conducted on the understanding that they had a home to which they could return. I envied them.

It was a crazy black American, Emile Leroi Wilson, from Watts, Los Angeles, who became my closest student friend. He burst like a bright firecracker on to the Oxford map, with his broad afro, half-mast checkered flares, gold-rimmed pebble glasses, and thin wiry 5 foot 7½ inch frame. A Rhodes Scholar studying for his doctorate on the life and Christian morality of Dr Martin Luther King, he had no qualms about introducing to his supervisor, and anyone else who might care to listen to him, terms such as jive-ass, dude, hip, cat, and funky. Somehow he managed to both restructure the vocabulary of half of Oxford, and still take his doctorate. My association with him began dramatically.

One day, while walking across the college front quad, I heard the porter shout at me. 'Mr Phillips! Mr Phillips!' I turned and walked back. He handed me a letter saying, 'This came for you, sir.' 'But it's addressed to Mr Wilson,' I pointed out. 'Well, where's Mr Wilson?' countered the porter. I gave him back the letter, shot him an irate glance, and left. Later that same day I was walking down Oxford High Street when I heard a voice behind me. 'Hey, my man!' I carried on walking, hoping that this did not mean me. The voice became exasperated. 'Hey you, motherfucker. You don't talk to black people or what? This place fuck up your head already. I hear you're taking my mail these days.' Mr Wilson was introducing himself.

To begin with Emile had nearly as much trouble under-standing me as I had trying to understand him. It was not just that he was eight years my senior. He seemed more con-fident, to have a cogent, if somewhat aggressive, idea of who he was and, as he would put it, where he was coming from. I found myself exhilarated by his company, but also panicking inside because I was so much less sure of myself. It was at this time that I started to travel to London to try, in Emile's

4

words, to 'plug into' black life. I would finish a tutorial, then catch the late morning train from Oxford to Paddington. Once there I would board a bus to Ladbroke Grove and arrive in time for a few drinks in any pub that was crowded with black people. After closing time I would wander about the Grove, then down to Shepherd's Bush. By early evening I would usually be 'hanging out' in Brixton. When it was too dark to observe in the streets, I wandered into pubs to listen to fictions being spluttered across the top of chipped beer mugs. Once or twice every term I would become embroiled in a good conversation and miss the last train back to Oxford. Unable to afford a hotel, I took the tube to Heathrow and slept in the Terminal 3 departure lounge. I was always back in Oxford by 9.30 the following morning, entering the lecture hall for 'Wyatt and Surrey: the sixteenth-century English lyric form', or whatever the morning topic might be.

My only other student activity was in drama. I nurtured the grandiose ambition of becoming a film director, but to start with I got involved with the theatre. In a short but intense fifteen-month period I directed six plays, including Pinter, Tennessee Williams, Shakespeare and Ibsen. Eventually the combination of theatre, my academic work, and most important of all, my secret trips to London, resulted in my collapsing with nervous exhaustion. I still had another year to go at Oxford, but I was drained. The college doctor insisted that I took a break and so, on the advice of one Emile Leroi Wilson, I decided to take up the offer of the advantageous air fares being advertised by Freddie Laker.

America meant little to me. Emile had 'sold' me the country as the sort of place where anybody could succeed given the right circumstances. But if you were not making it, he would say, you had every reason just to decide to take it. 'After all, the damn place was built on a revolution, and these days America is nothing more than a whole bunch of different tribes under the one presidential chief. And the brothers, we were the only ones who didn't want to come.

5

We got the damn right to complain to the white man until he wises up and says, "Yeah, I guess we did drag you here screaming and covered in shit".' Emile took great pleasure in pointing out that if you were a success in seventeenth- or eighteenth-century Europe the last place you would want to go would be the nothing colony of America. It was, in his opinion, a country built by a bunch of second raters with illegal slave labour.

After only a few days in New York I began to understand some of what he meant. Little Italy, Spanish Harlem, Chinatown, Harlem – the whole city seemed a testament to migratory patterns. I was stricken with the usual feelings that greet any visitor to New York – fear coupled with excitement. After a week I was ready to start exploring the rest of America. Within seventy-two hours of my departure I had been questioned by police in both Detroit and Chicago. Their reasoning seems as spurious now as it did then. All their questions centred on the simple fact that I was black and in the wrong street at the wrong time. In Atlanta the room service waiter warned me not to go out that evening as there was a Ku Klux Klan rally in town. In an Alabama hotel lobby, a woman confidently addressed me as 'boy', instructed me to carry her bags up to her room, and offered to tip me a dollar. By the time I reached Salt Lake City I was beginning to feel somewhat edgy about the whole venture.

Having arrived eventually in Salt Lake City at 5.30 a.m. and walked around for a couple of hours, I wandered into a downtown supermarket. I picked up a carton of orange juice and took it to the checkout counter. The man at the till served the woman in front of me and I watched her pack up her groceries into the familiar brown bag, and speed out of the shop into her waiting pick-up. Then the man proceeded to serve the woman behind me. Being a little slow, I thought it was a genuine mistake. 'Excuse me,' I re-proffered the carton but he continued to serve the woman behind me. The reality of my situation fell quietly upon me. I put down the carton, left the supermarket, and walked straight to the

Greyhound bus station. There was a three-hour wait for the bus to San Francisco, but I preferred to shelter from the streets of Salt Lake City. I bought an out-of-date copy of the *Los Angeles Times*, and settled into the number two berth in the queue. An hour or so later, I looked at my watch and started to plan what I would have to do when I returned to Oxford. Behind me, a hunch-shouldered man of about sixty leant forward to address the man in front of me, whom he had clearly never met before. 'Lot of niggers on the streets today.' The recipient of this information, who had earlier offered me a cigarette and borrowed my *Los Angeles Times*, looked horrified. 'In my day,' continued the man at my rear, 'if we saw too many niggers in the streets we'd shoot 'em.' My nominal ally ignored my nominal enemy. I burst out laughing. The absurd ritual of it all had finally reduced me to hysteria.

Five days later I was in Los Angeles. In fact, I was in a small town some thirty miles south of Los Angeles, but it is difficult to know where Los Angeles really ends. I was staying on a small cruiser moored in a marina. One day I took the bus into a nearby college town and found myself browsing in a book shop. A book called *Invisible Man* by Ralph Ellison caught my eye. I had already discovered what it meant to be invisible in America, but I bought it together with *Native Son* by Richard Wright. *Native Son* had a huge cover photograph of a young black man's face. The young man looked puzzled. I knew how he felt.

The next morning I woke early. I walked down to the beach with the Richard Wright book, and pointed my deck chair towards the Pacific. It was a warm, but not hot, early October day. The atmosphere was a little muggy, barely holding the heat. When I rose from the deck chair it was dark and I had finished my reading by moonlight. I felt as if an explosion had taken place inside my head. If I had to point to any one moment that seemed crucial in my desire to be a writer, it was then, as the Pacific surf began to wash up around the deck chair. The emotional anguish of the hero,

Bigger Thomas, the uncompromising prosodic muscle of Wright, his deeply felt sense of social indignation, provided not so much a model but a possibility of how I might be able to express the conundrum of my own existence. Even before I had opened Ralph Ellison's *Invisible Man*, I had decided that I wanted to try to become a writer.

Twenty-four hours after leaving California, I was once again sitting in an Oxford University lecture theatre. Physically I returned to my studies in better shape, but mentally I was shattered. My appetite for academic study was gone, and to make things worse it was the transitory season of autumn. I found myself sleeping during the summer-like days, and walking the streets during the winterish nights. Newspaper articles and the odd documentary on television were beginning to report the rebellious black youth 'problem'. I felt strongly that this was now the area which I wished to address, rather than the theories and counter-theories surrounding Shakespeare's 'problem' plays and Milton's later poetry. As far as the theatre was concerned, it too seemed increasingly irrelevant, and had nothing to do with the cultural or historical dilemma in which I found myself.

I went back to the college doctor, who told me that I was run down. 'Still?' I asked. 'These things take time,' he assured me, then prescribed Valium. My eyes seemed to be deteriorating so I went to the optician. 'Thought of changing from glasses to contact lenses?' he asked. So I began to wear contact lenses. But one question still loomed: what would I do when I finished my exams? I saw two clear paths. I could, as Derek Walcott put it, be inducted into 'white fellowships', be relatively secure, and move even further away from the vast majority of black people by pursuing an academic career. Alternatively, I could confront my own confusion and write. This path offered no security; I had little writing experience beyond a handful of teenage stories, and my tutor thought it 'rather reckless – stupid even'. Once again Emile came to my rescue, and strengthened my resolve by giving me a copy of Harold Cruse's pioneering study, *The Crisis of*

8

the Negro Intellectual. Despite the pompous and off-putting title, the contents helped me towards a decision.

I spent my last few weeks at Oxford resenting that it had taken America to make me conscious of my desire to write. This alone seemed to condemn the European Academy which had raised and educated me, and I found myself tediously attempting to question everything that I had ever been taught. The fundamental problem was, if I was going to continue to live in Britain, how was I to reconcile the contradiction of feeling British, while being constantly told in many subtle and unsubtle ways that I did not belong.

When my mother carried me away from the Caribbean in her arms we travelled to Britain by way of Italy and France. I had never been back to Europe but I knew now I would have to explore the European Academy that had shaped my mind. A large part of finding out who I was, and what I was doing here, would inevitably mean having to understand the Europeans. I could not believe that the British were really any different from the French, or the Spanish from the Swedish. All these different nationalities were to be found in college, plus many others. They all seemed to share a common and mutually inclusive, but culturally exclusive culture. Reorientating myself in Britain seemed spurious; the problem was a European one, as exemplified by the shared, twisted, intertwined histories of the European countries.

Before I explored Europe there was one other journey I felt compelled to make: the journey back to the Caribbean of my birth. The discoveries that I made there were both deep and profound, but I still felt like a transplanted tree that had failed to take root in foreign soil. The direction in which my branches had grown still puzzled me, for the forces that had shaped their development were not to be found in the Caribbean. I found this disturbing, as I hoped that the Caribbean might furnish me with answers to urgently felt questions. In fact, all that happened was that my Caribbean journey heightened an already burning desire to increase my awareness of Europe and Europeans.

Hollywood's Casablanca

Casablanca is one of those rare cities, mention it and people immediately feel envious of your plans to visit a place they seem to know so well. The city has been ensnared, like Acapulco and Rio de Janeiro, by the more glamorous tentacles of media colonization. However, its present-day African reality and the image the world has of it bear little resemblance to each other.

At Heathrow reality began to intrude. In all Third World countries travel, from the dusty battered bus to the seemingly slickest of airlines, is uniformly chaotic. Royal Air Maroc seemed to operate on the assumption that if every seat is full then some passengers can squeeze up and make new friends. I sat behind three girls, students who were returning from a month's 'study' in London. They were loudly screeching a medley of hits by an English band called Frankie Goes to Hollywood. To my left sat Kareem. He wore glasses and looked much too studious for his nineteen years. Dressed simply in well-ironed cotton, his olive skin looked as though it had been freshly oiled. He began a five-hour monologue. I had always imagined there must be a limit to what one could say about first-division soccer. As the plane landed Kareem finished reading the emergency instructions and touched my arm. 'Welcome to Africa,' he whispered. My hands twitched as I suppressed violent thoughts.

I had flown into a kingdom. At Muhammad V Airport (named after the father of the present king, Hassan II), security was tight. Armed policemen littered the tarmac. On entering the arrivals lounge I became part of a melting pot of blacks, Arabs and whites. Behind me a Jewish man in a black hat, who would not have looked out of place in a Woody Allen film, chose from his many passports. To my left a huge neon-lit sign superimposed a mosque over the message, 'American Express welcomes you to Morocco.' Then Kareem reappeared. He managed to confuse matters by telling the passport officer that I was a journalist rather than a writer, then deserted me for his father whom he greeted French-style with a kiss on each cheek. Having finally talked my way into the country, I found myself in the jurisdiction of a tall Moroccan soldier with clean, sharp eyes and a bright face. He informed me that he had been assigned to 'help', and did so by steering me towards the bus for the city centre, which lay some twelve kilometres away from the airport. My enquiries about currency, newspapers and hotels all drew a smiling blank. 'Help' meant getting arrivals out of the airport terminal as quickly as possible.

My first night in Africa passed peacefully enough. No spears whistled over my head, no lions roared in the distance. Only the odd car rubbering by in the boulevard below and the hum of the air-conditioning disturbed my sleep. In the morning, at an international newspaper stand, I met my first Moroccan friend, Muhammad. He was thirty, small and thin like a snake. His eyes protruded slightly to give the impression of poverty, and I soon believed he could bulge them at will. His brown suit had flared bottoms, and his yellow shirt was open-collared and grubby. I was sure that the rest of his wardrobe was Moroccan, and that when he reached home he quickly slipped out of these ill-fitting Western clothes. Muhammad peered around the corner of my *Times* and claimed that he recognized me from the hotel, where he worked. He then told me that he had just taken the day off as he was sick. In his next sentence Muhammad had taken the day off because Abdul, his five-year-old son, was sick. 'And what's the name of our hotel?' I asked. He skipped this question, pretending his English was not good enough to cope with it. There was a moment's silence. Then he piped up, 'Maybe we take a small tour, yes?' And so began the

Muhammad 'rap' as together we walked around 'the white city' of 2 million inhabitants. 'Brother this . . . brother that . . . and what colour is your wife?' 'I don't have a wife.' 'But she'll be black like you, won't she?' 'Maybe. Maybe not.' 'White people are full of shit, *n'est-ce pas*?' Muhammad had the patter, but no money. As he trailed me through the shops, it soon became clear that I wanted neither wallets nor bags, hashish nor leather jackets, from all of which he would have received a kick-back. It was then that he started to worry about his nice tip, yes? Muhammad thought 100 to 150 dirhams (£10 to £15) would be in order. His words drummed on deaf ears. I gave him fifty dirhams which he gratefully accepted.

Casablanca is to hustling what New York is to sky-scrapers. 'You want hash?' hissed shady-looking men who appeared out of every nook and cranny. 'You want good shit?' And the romance of seeing a group of hooded Berbers gliding down a street was soon offset by the sight of the many beggarwomen. Bundled up in shop doorways or on the sidewalk itself, babies sucking at their large, dry breasts, the women's hands jutted out like stiff obstacles, fingers stretched, palms bare, often asleep or buried under their mound of children. The smell and noise of Casablanca became overpowering. The flies were a constant menace, potential illness was a pressing concern. Everywhere there were hordes of wandering pariah-like dogs and flea-ridden cats. Outside the medians the water-carriers sold water that I found difficult to believe anyone would want to drink. In order to escape the clamour of the street I made the inevitable trip into the Kasbah, which turned out to be like entering the inner circle of hell. The further in, the more frantic the hustling and the harder it becomes to remember how to get out. The streets become narrower, shops smaller, voices higher. The offers of hash double, and the voices recognizing you as an intruder become bolder. 'Hey, Joe!' 'Hey, Jim!' Hashish is, of course, the ultimate Moroc-can tourist trap, guaranteeing five to ten years in gaol, with no remission, if you are caught in possession.

I escaped the Kasbah and passed back out into the fume-intoxicated streets, where a crowd of waifs began to follow me. They have learnt, as part of their language, to contort their faces into the most pathetic plea for help – a simpering moan, a quivering bottom lip, watering eyes, head lolling to one side like that of a dog – and they managed to position themselves so I had to look down on them, as though they had tucked themselves under an imaginary wing. It occurred to me that everyone was watching, but they were not, for this was a tragically familiar scene. Eventually, if you do not give in, they disappear to hold on to another sucker's waistband-conscience. This was not the dazzling Casablanca that I had been expecting. This big-business city, with its clean concrete and glass, right-angled, leather-briefcased, airline-companied order, existed and functioned in the face of disorder, under-development and unimaginable misery. It attracted poverty from the desert and hills and, like so many Third World cities, created an even more depraved urban poverty. The two faces of Casablanca appeared to be so happily married that it was as though each needed to feel the proximity of the other to be sure of its status. As though beauty and order were increased in direct proportion to the level of surrounding squalor. And poverty became more bearable the greater the evidence of potential escape to wealth.

Some days later I happened across a young European Inter-Railing couple. Their confusion, and their resulting conversation, sounded familiar. I had overheard it in the voices of at least half a dozen different couples in sidewalk cafés throughout the city. They were both long-haired, haversacked, sandalled, and clinging to a tight budget and fat guide book. Each sipped a Coke, packs bulging up against the table as if both they and their owners were awaiting a camel. Their straws poked out of the top of shapely bottles, and they looked cautiously towards the Kasbah. 'Are we going in?' he asked. 'Whose idea was this?' she replied. He knew that he was to blame, but countered with the fact that he managed to get some dope last night. 'Isn't that something?' 'That dirty old man who tried to get you stoned so he could take all our money and have his way with me? He couldn't take his eyes off my tits.' Her companion sighed audibly as she continued. 'And don't say I should wear a bra. It's hot in Morocco and . . .'

The heat and dust were overwhelming, the noise of the traffic and the vendors plying their trade continued until late into the night on the crowded sidewalks. In the day the more prosperous suburbs of Casablanca were a magnificent sight stretching away on the horizon, white squares of different sizes reflecting the sun and casting dramatic shadows in all directions. The houses were like blocks of chalk with holes cut into them for windows. This richer face was like a model for an ideal desert city that nobody had yet painted. Down by the harbour the landscape became more functional. The port of Casablanca was dominated by a medley of cranes, a crop of metallic erections towering over vast rusting bulks called *Aegean Wind* or *African Spirit*, ships that could sail the Atlantic on a breeze despite their size. Beside them, and stacked in untidy piles, were huge container boxes, like giant forgotten letters, each a different colour (mucky brown, off green, dull red, chipped black, damaged grey) sporting a variety of coded addresses. Each evening I heard the Muslim call to prayer pierce the air, like a lone wolf howling on a dark night. Nobody seemed to move to answer it.

On the walk back to my hotel the appeals began again. I rapidly lost patience with the hustlers. 'Haven't you bastards got any self-respect?' In their vocabulary 'dignity' had been reduced to a small word in high-heeled shoes. They smiled, dropped their shoulders and giggled slightly. I noted that beggars were all ages. Hustlers were generally under thirty-five, and I wondered if the lame had been reduced to begging by losing a leg or an arm in a back-street game of chance. Did retired hustlers with limbs intact become taxi-drivers? As I strolled on my Moroccan buddies continued to call to me.

'Hey, brother!' 'Hey, friend!' I concentrated hard on cultivating an air of indifference. But I was lost and, against my better judgement, I asked someone the way back to the hotel. The golden rule is never to believe a word that a Moroccan street-boy utters. He will say anything to make you happy so that he might get a tip and a chance to practise his English – anything in reply to the most absurd requests. Q: What time does the *Titanic* leave? A: One o'clock, my friend. It's best to go to an agency for a ticket. I can show you the way. What's your name? Mine is Farrukh. Or, Q: Can you tell me where I can get *Apollo 13* to the moon? A: Ah, you are American. I have been to the moon, too, so I can show you the way, my brother. You like Morocco? You want a B girl and champagne? Street talk can induce a nervous breakdown in seconds.

The truth of Morocco's current predicament is startlingly depressing. According to the World Bank, 12 million of Morocco's 25 million people live below the poverty line. A fifth of the population inhabits shanty towns around the main cities, one in five is unemployed, and a large percentage of children between the ages of seven and twelve are exploited in small manufacturing establishments and mines, working ten-hour days for food and lodgings. There is no unemployment pay, virtually no social insurance, and while wages have been frozen for two years, the cost of living has doubled and the annual rate of inflation risen to over 20 per cent. In recent years the only people to receive a pay increase have been Government ministers, who have more than doubled their own salaries. The World Health Organization (WHO) rates the Moroccan health system as among the worst in the world. Everything has to be paid for including bandages and syringes. Since independence from France in 1956, the kingdom has had four popular uprisings that have been brutally suppressed by the 200,000-strong armed forces. Now, with drought becoming an urgent problem, electricity and water prices spiralling, and the bottom falling out of the world value of phosphate, the country's major resource, the $11 billion foreign debt can only grow.

King Hassan II's response has been predictable: the deflection of discontent away from the domestic arena towards the nationalistic pursuit of a foreign war. Since Morocco's annexation of the abandoned Spanish Western Sahara in 1975, the country has been at war with the rebels of the Polisario Front. The Front is recognized by sixty-one countries, by the Organization of African Unity (OAU) – of which Morocco is no longer a member – and by the Non-Aligned Movement. Apart from a recently signed agreement with oil-rich Libya, who needs cheap Moroccan labour, Morocco is almost isolated politically. The United States have continued to cultivate links with Morocco only so that they can exploit her strategic position for the US Mediterranean fleet. However, the rest of the world looks askance at Morocco, and her people are beginning to realize this.

At the start of 1985 over 200 Moroccans were killed in 'domestic disturbances'. There is increasing evidence that Hassan's foreign 'adventure' can no longer disguise the serious crisis at the heart of the nation. Clearly the $2 billion spent annually on this fruitless war could be put to better use in a country whose illiteracy rate of 65 per cent helps maintain the 'strong' king's popularity. Like so many African countries, independence has brought only a further crippling dependency upon multinational companies, and has allowed the colonial collaborators to step forth as petty neo-colonial despots. *France Soir* and *Le Matin* are still widely read, and the French colonial past lingers on in the names of the streets, although some like Place de France have changed – it is now Place Muhammad V. But the progress is largely superficial.

In today's *Casablanca* Humphrey Bogart's Rick would have spent all day throwing babied beggars out of his Café Américain. In the street the Moroccans would have offered piano-playing Sam a joint and assumed that he was a Sudanese or Senegalese. 'Hey, Sam, you want hash?' The

Casablanca bar of the Hyatt Regency Hotel is a museum to the Warner Brothers film of the same name. As I sat down I wondered how many Moroccans had actually seen the film. I knew not many had seen this bar: at £3 for a small bottle of Heineken its prices were prohibitive. Low voices eased across the bar like a desert wind. Women, their faces plastered with rouge as though somebody had slapped them, waited for encounters, unconcerned about the permanence of relationships. The walls laboured under the weight of posters and stills – Bergman, Bogart, Henreid, Claude Rains, Sidney Greenstreet. Director – Michael Curtiz. Producer – Hal B. Wallis. In this tinted-glass, temperature-controlled atmosphere I felt as cut off from Morocco as Rick must have been. When the waiter returned with a small bowl of peanuts I asked him if he had seen the film. 'Yes,' he said. 'At a special showing in the hotel cinema.' Did he like it? *'Oui, mais ce n'est pas Morocco.'*

Rick's Café Américain, like the Hyatt Regency with its tall lobby, red carpets, piped music and fez-topped porters, could certainly have existed. But it is a demonstration of Hollywood's power that she was able to manufacture a film set against the backdrop of humanity's greatest war, and in a country under the jackboot of colonialism, which gave such a distorted view of a city and a people. As time has gone by, I am sure that very little in Hollywood has changed, and if there were profit to be made Warner Brothers would remake *Casablanca* set in a Hyatt Regency with Michael Jackson singing songs to Jack Nicholson's command, and Meryl Streep playing the lead female interest. But that still leaves the question of who will play Muhammad, or the one-legged beggar, or the woman who tried to give me her child? The same invisible people who played them in *Casablanca*, perhaps.

Why the film continues to exercise a grip on the collective consciousness of generation after generation of movie-goers still puzzles me. Quickly thrown together in 1942 by a group of on-the-line professionals under the guidance of the

Hungarian director Michael Curtiz, politically the film is crude propaganda for the Allies. In fact, with hindsight, parts of it can even be considered offensive. Can we really believe now that Paul Henreid, dapper in a Savile Row suit, has been released from a concentration camp? And when Ingrid Bergman describes the middle-aged Dooley Wilson as 'the boy who's playing piano' a shiver runs both ways along my spine. But perhaps the film's success lies in its continuing emotional appeal. From the classic scene where they all belt out 'La Marseillaise' with the Nazis present, to the Bogart–Rains conclusion on the tarmac ('Louis, this could be the start of a beautiful friendship'), the film's emotional intensity and idealistic naïvety blend perfectly and create a powerfully optimistic thesis, and a blueprint for American involvement in the Second World War. Hollywood's ability to leap deftly even the greatest hurdles of reality and create myths independent of place, time and facts, will always be its greatest strength.

Leaving the Hyatt Regency, I went to see *Rocky II* at the Empire Cinema on rue Muhammad V. Rocky Balboa, the Italian Stallion out of Philadelphia, versus Apollo Creed, a black American out of somewhere in Africa, once removed. The crowd cheered and stomped in approval at Balboa's highly improbable and ridiculously romantic victory. Then they poured out into the humid midnight air. Hollywood still works. On a hot sweaty African night, in a packed cinema on the main drag of Casablanca, a night of teeth, eyes, glistening brows, and shadowy agitation, the people were literally on the edge of their seats for Stallone. If I did not already know that he had directed and written the movie too, I would have imagined Stallone to be an extra from *One Flew Over The Cuckoo's Nest*. I was now anxious to leave Casablanca.

The shanty towns on the edge of the city are made up from bits of wood and iron, dried mud baked by the sun, and sticks and twigs to reinforce walls and establish boundaries. The people live in these small square tinderboxes and try to scratch a living out of stony brown soil. There is no shade. Dogs and children run wild, sheep are herded into a loose cluster, and these houses, which from a distance look like inverted pots, are too low to stand up in. At this, the frayed edges of the city, the only organized enclaves are the cemeteries. People walk aimlessly alongside railway tracks, the two iron rails being the only sign of a sense of direction in the environment. These little wattle shanty towns reminded me of the Caribbean, of people locked in a cycle of poverty where to own a bicycle is not so much a sign of wealth as evidence of a potential bid for freedom. Any escape through athletic prowess is out of the question, for where is the food to nourish the body? And academic achievement can be discounted, as an extra pair of hands scratching at stubble means an extra mouth can be fed. Beside a donkey and a cart, the owner lay folded asleep on the ground. The donkey's tail swished lazily from side to side and shooed away the flies, and the landscape repeats itself for miles.

In the airport I walked from the coffee bar without paying the bill after I saw a mouse run unseen by anyone across the bar top. Maybe others noticed and were just ignoring it as commonplace. In the departure lounge I heard the snatches of conversation that usually depress me. England always begins too soon. This time I listened carefully, curious to know how others had responded to the city. 'And the smell going through that Kasbah – like a sweet spicy smell. Janice was right not to want to eat there, by heck.' 'Well, it was either *France Soir* or my hand in that lav. What else could I do?' Then, with swinging Polaroids, clutching Kasbah treasure and two bottles of duty-free, my acquaintances leapt into a lively discussion about whether sunglasses are needed in the evening. My mind fled back a month to the South of France. I had been sitting having lunch in a restaurant in St Paul de Vence with the American writer James Baldwin. La Colombe d'Or is the sort of place where people spend more time looking at each other than at the menu. Baldwin, being a local resident and possessing a very distinctive face, was clearly an object of some attention. And, inevitably, the waitress appeared with a message. She knew Baldwin very well, but she still had to ask. 'Mrs Roger Moore would like to know if you are the gentleman who played piano in *Casablanca*?' Baldwin and I laughed, as did the waitress. As my 'acquaintances' decided that sunglasses were 'a boon' in the evening, I laughed again.

Britain's Gibraltar

You'll also receive a warm welcome from the people of Gibraltar, because just like you, we're British. (We speak English and deal in pounds and pence, so there's no 'Language Barrier' or 'Mickey Mouse' money problems to worry about.)

Gibraltar Tourist Board leaflet

'Gibraltar' is a corruption of the Arabic words *Jebel* Tariq, meaning Tariq's mountain. It was named after the Moor Tariq ibn Zeyad who commanded the capture of Gibraltar in AD 711. It measures three miles by one mile, boasts a population of 30,000, and lies at the point where Europe almost kisses Africa. In 1713 the Treaty of Utrecht officially assigned this large finger, which juts out from the southern coast of Spain and points the way towards Tangier, to the British. Were it to be amputated Spain would have a nice smooth coastline.

Gibraltar is a geographical anomaly. It is dominated by a rock that rises steeply on all sides to 1,300 feet. This oval wart stretches from the knuckle of the finger to the edge of the fingernail. The people live squeezed up between the sea and the cliff faces. Where this finger meets the hand is the frontier with Spain. It is only from the air that the extent to which this promontory is dominated by 'the Rock' becomes clear.

The 'Welcome to RAF Gibraltar' sign at the airport prepares the visitor. The food at the hotel, flat, grey and leathery, confirms that this is 'Britain'. The colonial ladies whose table I shared were brogued and wore two-piece Crimplene suits. They looked contemptuously at the Spanish waiters, reducing them to clumsiness. I looked down and realized that my meal had been served on off-white Pyrex school regulation crockery. The after-dinner coffee was of the do-it-yourself variety; a jug of hot water and a sachet of powder. I retired to the lounge. The hotel took the *Daily Telegraph* and the *Daily Express*. 'No, of course we don't have any other papers, Mr Phillips.' The proprietress was full of over-scented charm. I went up to my room to watch television.

Gibraltar Broadcasting Corporation (GBC) feeds the populace a diet of ice-skating exhibitions, old police serials that feature actors most of whom have since died, *The Big Match* (which is Saturday's soccer shown on Tuesday), and documentaries imported from Britain with titles such as *The Sea In Their Blood*. They refer to the British in the third person, 'They live not more than eighty miles from the sea . . . building ships is more a way of life, than a means for them to make a living . . .' The station signs off with the Queen inspecting her Household Cavalry during the Trooping of the Colour ceremony. It is followed by the test card, which is suspiciously similar to that used by the BBC, just the one letter avoiding a breach of copyright.

The GBC morning news is a curious mixture of the global – a hijacking in Columbia – and the British – the miners' strike, inflation, cricket scores – with those affairs that are close to the Gibraltarean heart. These items included a man who locked himself in a cave all night to raise money for a gardening society, an inquiry into why a local basketball match did not happen, and the exciting announcement that Miss P. Wigley saw three dolphins this morning off the end of the Rock. For those still hungry for more indigenous information, this is followed by the local *Notice Board* which is: 'This evening in the church hall there will be a meeting of the Diabetics on the Rock Association.' Then the highlight of the morning's entertainment, excerpts from the BBC's *Fawlty Towers* series, which is about as diplomatic as the BBC Africa Service broadcasting *Little Black Sambo*. Mañuel, the idiotic waiter from Barcelona, is the 'star' of the situation comedy. He is simply a crude figure of fun for the British to mock.

The main street of Gibraltar reminded me of any small inland English town, with its parade of well-known chain stores jostling with the smaller gift shops, tobacconists, butchers, jewellers and chemists. The odd 'bobby' is on the beat. Besides the weather, the only signs that this is not England, are yesterday's newspapers on the stands and the occasional Spanish conversations that pepper the air. The social spectrum of British people tends to be wide, ranging from the 'Hooray Henry' upper classes connected with the military – and dapper in tweeds despite temperatures of 26 degrees Celsius – to the tourists who begin conversations by saying, 'All right, Tel? Sandra reckons you forgot your camera at Gatwick.' Their cartoon-like faces were almost Hogarthian, their bodies best summarized as two legs and two arms in search of a suntan, until, exposed to the sun, they merely squint and flee for cover. The tourists were nearly always badly dressed in tops that did not quite match the bottoms, or clad simply in Union Jack shorts. Theoretically the permanent population includes a specifically ethnic Gibraltarean who is a mixture of Jewish, Genoese, Maltese, Arab, British and Spanish, and speaks Yanito, a Hispanicized form of the English language. But the truth is that most people sound and look Western European. British, in fact.

In Gibraltar people drive on the left-hand side of the road. The Spanish and Moroccans view this behaviour with the vague and amused sense of detachment that British socio-cultural aggression often provokes. Most bars seemed to be overly decorated with military insignia, pool tables, juke boxes, Pac-man machines, and one-armed bandits. 'Dimple mug or straight glass?' was the familiar British response to my asking for a pint of lager. Ordering food appeared to be equally complicated. 'Ross or Birds Eye fish fingers, sir?', the ludicrous assumption being that there is a discernible difference between the two. The pub next door had the added 'attraction' of 'race by race' commentaries from English racecourses. The menu exemplified the height of British cuisine. 'We do Kebabs and Popadoms.' The shop across the road 'did' fish and chips (wrapped up in the *Sun*) for those who sought variety. I did not. The barmaid pulled another pint and reached for a calculator. 'Persayters is it, love?' I left the bar only to discover that in Gibraltar a copy of the *Observer* at £1.50 costs three times the price of twenty cigarettes.

To the west of Gibraltar the industrial chimneys of Algeciras belch smoke that rises arrow-like, before thinning and drifting aimlessly. The harbour is rich with oil slicks, the liquid debris of industrialization. From the top of the Rock I could see every boat for miles, from the smallest yacht with a scrap of rag for a sail to a Saudi tanker. The big naval cruisers were surrounded by smaller private boats which were being washed with loving care by their owners in a manner that reminded me of the British suburban habit of washing the car on a Sunday. Nothing could escape my gaze. Gibraltar's existence denies Spain a decent look-out point. Tarifa, away to the west although further south, sees the Atlantic-bound traffic after Gibraltar. Unless ships pass by Gibraltar under cover of night, the British will see them. Lloyds of London maintain a monitoring post here. From their look-out station at Europa Point, it is possible to see Africa lying to the front, Spain behind, the Mediterranean to the east, and the Atlantic to the west. There is no better place to watch the world's business go floating by. It is also an easy stronghold to defend, for the east and west faces of the Rock are sheer, the south is impossible. At the summit there is a plaque to commemorate a Spanish shepherd who in 1704 led 500 Spanish soldiers up the east face, only to be discovered by a British garrison. The difficulty of the failed enterprise elicits even British acknowledgement.

Looking out across the Straits of Gibraltar on a clear day, Africa appears to be a small symmetrical island rising in the centre to a high summit. Europeans could have imagined it as just that, an island. A thin circle of cirrus cloud makes a halo just below the peaks of the Rif mountains to the east of Tangier. Back on the Rock, Barbary apes run wild. There are about fifty of them, a yard in length, and their continued presence is a result of superstition. It is rumoured that if the apes leave the Rock the British will follow. Tame, and now used to playing with tourists for titbits of food, they sometimes snatch a handbag or a pair of glasses to keep up the pretence of being wild.

After fourteen recorded sieges across the years it does not take a genius to realize that Gibraltar is primarily a military zone. It is not only a NATO base, but a location for the storage of nuclear weapons. Every Monday the Duke of Wellington's Regiment (West Riding) perform the 'Ceremonial changing of the Guard in front of the Convent, residence of His Excellency the Governor', at 10.20 a.m. precisely. The Governor, his wife, daughter and son royally salute from their balcony. A real, live military tattoo takes place with clockwork precision despite soaring temperatures. Large groups of tourists applaud excessively at the end of each manoeuvre, and before and during the event one very shrewd soldier sells pre-recorded tapes of the proceedings. As this amusing commercial performance drew to a close I found myself wandering off in the direction of Trafalgar Cemetery. It is small, shady, and as discreet as any cemetery in the middle of a town can ever hope to be. The atmosphere is both peaceful and moving. The dead from three crucial 'Naval actions of His Majesty's Forces' are buried here – Trafalgar (October, 1805), Cadiz (May, 1810), and Malaga (April, 1812). A short distance away are the very elegant Alameda Gardens where old Spaniards sit and listen to Spanish programmes on their transistors. They look out longingly over Algeciras.

Back at the hotel the proprietress apologized about the noise in the street. 'You know what the Spanish are like.' I assumed she meant that like any other people, they shout, play radios loudly, drive motorbikes that need their exhausts repaired, and blow their car horns. If so, then I knew the

Spanish well. Except these 'Spanish' seemed to have an exceptional grasp of colloquial English. The anti-Spanish fervour of the Gibraltareans bordered on the ridiculous. Comments on prospective Spanish sovereignty ranged from, 'Where will we go?', to 'The Spanish will make a shit-hole of it.' The hotel proprietress made it her business to warn me that should I stay too long in the border town of La Linea I would be robbed, raped and heaven knows what else. She also proffered the information that Moroccans were dirty people. Their 'unfortunate' arrival had coincided with the 1969 closing of the border when it became more difficult for the Spanish to commute. Before the Moroccans came, she claimed the Gibraltareans used to hose the streets clean three times a day. Morning, siesta-time, and at night. Now nobody bothered. She gave me the key to my room and found something else to do when I asked her why 'they' didn't still hose the streets.

As Gibraltar approaches its fourth century of British rule, the attitude of the colonizers is becoming increasingly stubborn. There is a real fear of the imagined wave of 'immigrants', be they Spanish or Moroccan, who will arrive once the border with Spain is permanently re-opened. The 6 per cent unemployment rate is spiralling, and only thirteen weeks' unemployment benefit is payable. Across the frontier in La Linea 10,000 are unemployed, while the situation is even more acute all over Andalucía. As a new member of the Common Market, Spain desperately needs access to the European labour pool, and it is likely that after the seven-year transitional period, when there is free movement of labour across all Common Market frontiers, Gibraltar's British identity will be swallowed up. Naturally, the Spaniards will start by filling what job vacancies there are in Gibraltar, although if the military were to pull out there would be precious few of these, for 60 per cent of Gibraltar's 17,000 jobs come via the Ministry of Defence. But irrespective of whether the military pull out or what the average Gibraltarean thinks, it will only be a matter of time before the

Spanish press home a full claim for sovereignty, and re-integrate Gibraltar into mainland Spain. I listened to a woman in a bar lamenting the fact that there were only 'seven hotels on the island'. Somebody pointed out that Gibraltar was not an island, and that despite the royally inscribed red pillar boxes the Cathedral, like many in Andalucía, was an ex-mosque. Gibraltar has a Spanish history that long predates the British presence. The conversation was interrupted by the GBC weather report. 'Today in London it was 26 degrees, on the Rock we had a high of 29 degrees, in Manchester it was 24 degrees . . .' Induced by colonialism, Gibraltar's schizophrenia continues to be fed by the stubbornness of colonial pride.

Britain is in an impasse: she cannot pull out of Gibraltar any more than she can the Falklands, Northern Ireland or Hong Kong. She has a 'duty' to these people who continue to live on patches of colonial soil. Unlike the black people of Africa, Asia and the Caribbean, who demanded independence, these people are saying, 'We do not want it.' Britain remains their lifeline – they cling and hold. The thought of being pushed away from their cultural watering hole engenders panic. Close to the Spanish frontier there is a pleasant little triangular garden where a stone memorial has been engraved with the words, In Glorious Memory of those who died for Empire. This monumental stone was for me the Rock of Gibraltar. Spain's entry into the Common Market will eventually push Gibraltar into a new era – the twentieth century.

A pagan Spain

I'm a self-conscious Negro and I'm the product of Western Culture, living with white people far from my racial origins. I began to ask myself how did I get there, who brought me there and why? What kind of people were they who dared the oceans to get slaves and sell them? It was in Spain . . . that I found my answers.

Richard Wright, *Pagan Spain*, 1957

My first view of Spain was of a flotilla of rusting hulks. This was the harbour of Algeciras. I disembarked, then watched as the ship on which I had arrived turned towards Tangier leaving a furrowed road in its wake. I hailed a taxi and asked the driver if he spoke English. '*Habla inglés?*' 'The funny thing is', he began lighting a cigarette, 'I survive all these years in Spain just speaking Spanish.' His sardonic wit was Liverpudlian in style. There was nothing much in Algeciras, apart from the familiar fellers hanging around the street corners asking if I wanted hash, a hotel, or a whore – in that order. The waterfront was dominated by travel agents, eating places and cheap hotels. A brisk walk confirmed my suspicions that Algeciras was simply a port tacked on to an indifferent city. Civilization, in the form of wheel–clamps, had taken hold, but there were no tourist sights to trouble my eyes. When the lights go down in Algeciras people go to bed. It all seemed reasonably simple and straightforward.

On my way back to the once grandiloquent and romantic, now slightly faded, Hotel Reina Christina, I bumped into a group of a dozen or so boys. They were aged between seven and thirteen and all asked me for a cigarette. I did not know what they meant so they showed me with the universal puffing gesture. Laughing, I told them I did not smoke. They laughed. For a moment I was sure they did not believe me. Then one of the boys jammed the smallest boy's hand up against my arm, and they all noticed that his skin colour vaguely resembled mine. Again they all laughed. 'He is', announced their leader, his finger wagging accusingly at the small boy, *'un negro.'* *'Ah, dos negros. Un grande negro y un pequeño negro,'* observed another boy. Everybody, myself included, laughed. The boy was not black, just the possessor of a slightly tanned skin, centuries of Jewish, gypsy, Moorish, Arab and European blood surging through his young veins. His distinctive, slightly hooked nose, his wide black eyes, were like their own. His skin alone marked him out as different, although he was as Spanish as they were. I ruffled the small boy's hair, and recognizing his Barcelona soccer shirt told them all that Barcelona were useless, and that Real Madrid were the only team in Spain. They looked at me as though I had personally insulted each of them in turn. I backed down, and later that year they were to be proved right as Barcelona went on to win the Spanish league. Despite our argument, we remained friends and talked on. An hour passed and dusk fell. They wanted to know if I was going to sleep at the hotel. They made babyish goodnight gestures by tilting their heads to one side, and sliding their pressed palms up beside their ears. Then one of the boys began to play with my digital watch. I showed him how to set it, let him try, retrieved the watch, then left. *'Adiós, amigos!'* *'Adiós, el señor negro!'*

The following day I stopped my hired car on a hillside so that I might look at the view over Tarifa. I got out and strolled a short distance down the hill. There I met an old man whose haggard face looked like an unmade bed. He shared his bread and cheese with me, although his mule looked better fed than he did. Like most Spaniards he possessed a stern dignity and considered himself a *caballero*, any man's equal, and a gentleman. We sat and looked out over

Africa and conducted a discussion about Franco, the Moors, and the British, the major part of it in sign language. He told me that he did not consider Marbella a part of Spain any more. I would later discover why. I deduced from his conversation that at some point he had been to Germany or Switzerland (or both) as a migrant worker. And then our exchange ended as naturally as it had begun. The town over which we gazed is the most southerly in Europe. Like Sagres – in neighbouring Portugal the port from which Vasco da Gama set sail – Tarifa feels like the end of the world. We both looked down and listened to the roar of the Atlantic as it pounded up against a huge man-made breakwater. Behind it the Mediterranean lapped contentedly. I stood up, thanked the man, and walked back up the hill to my car.

Tarifa boasts an old Moorish castle, but few beaches of any consequence. Tourism is minimal. At the end of the breakwater there is a military base. A red and white barrier barred my path. *Entrada Prohibido. Zona Militar.* A policeman looked at me as though daring me to trespass. Back on the mainland, and looking out over the harbour and across to Africa, there is a statue of the Virgin Mary. Its message is addressed to the infidel North Africans. Simply, 'Don't try it on again, pal.' Eight centuries of Moorish and Arab civilization distinguishes Spain's early history from the rest of Europe. The evidence of this can be seen in the extraordinary architecture of Muslim statement and Christian-inspired counter-statement, particularly in Seville, Granada, and Spain's Muslim capital, Córdoba. Spanish Islam meant that at a time when most of Europe was backward by comparison, Córdoba had a population of half a million, who quoted poetry from a library of 400,000 books, strolled well-paved streets, and worshipped in one of the 500 mosques in this 'Athens of the West'. Meanwhile, London was being besieged by Viking bandits and Paris was nothing more than an island fortress.

Some half an hour's drive up the west coast from Tarifa, and about ten miles inland, I found the tiny Andalucian village of Vjer de la Frontera. It is a startling sight, an official

Spanish monument, perched away up on a hilltop and flood-lit at night. Every house is white and they are all clustered together as if seeking protection. In the afternoon I walked freely and saw nobody, hearing only the noises of late lunch. Through narrow lanes, past grilled and shuttered windows, I paused to admire the tiled entrances that were invariably thick with potted and hanging plants. The village was open and invitingly cool, but the people were hidden away. A snatch of jabbered conversation is all that I received, wandering till lost in the maze of streets. Then I heard an old Spanish guitar and stopped to listen. I was unsure if it was a bar or a house that the bright curtain concealed, such is the private informality of this village. I began to thread my way out of the peaceful labyrinth, listening for street voices or a car engine, the rattling of keys or the hoarse machine-gunning of a punctured exhaust on a teenager's Honda. Eventually I reached the village square and sat down for a rest. It was dominated by an impressive marbled fountain. This village 'square' was circular and around its perimeter marble benches with wrought-iron backs alternated with palms. Everyone had front row seats, and was able to stare at the fountain, which, as the day faded away, assumed the shrouded antiquity of an altarpiece.

Spain is a beautiful and large country, second only to the Soviet Union in Europe. Of all its disparate parts Andalucía is probably the best known, the most often written about, and the most romantic. The climate is good, food and drink cheap, so it has always attracted writers from Robert Graves to Ernest Hemingway, Chester Himes to Laurie Lee. The people's chiselled features are immediately distinctive, and the pitch-black garb of the Spanish duenna, offset only by the blood-red rose, is the most severe but also the finest of all national costumes. These colours seem to characterize Spain's proud and regal spirit. It is in Andalucía, where these costumes abound, that one can feel Moorish Spain at its most insistent. The defeat of the Moors in 1492 coincided exactly with Columbus's first voyage. Spain lost her Islamic face and her Jewish population, which was either expelled or persecuted to death by the Inquisition, but gained a great overseas empire. According to V. S. Pritchett they were 'the sixteenth and seventeenth century . . . master-race of the world, the founders of the first great Empire to succeed the Roman Empire'. Spain's expansionist desires were nurtured in the struggle of the *Reconquista* – the centuries-long battle between the crescent and the cross. Soldier married saint, state married religion, in order to defeat the infidel. This unholy marriage survives until the present day. Everywhere I turned I seemed to see either a church or a military uniform. And although people maintain that since Franco's demise in 1975 Spain has changed, the spirit of soldier and saint still seemed overpowering.

'*Viva* Tejoro' was daubed across walls prominently enough to suggest that the graffito was there with the collusion of the local authorities. Colonel Tejoro led the army's storming of the Spanish Parliament in 1981. For eighteen hours the new Spanish democracy teetered on a knife-edge until King Juan Carlos made a dramatic televised speech to the nation denouncing Tejoro. Simmering Fascism by no means constitutes the full extent of Spain's contemporary problems. ETA, the guerrilla arm of the Basque separatist movement, is waging a campaign against the Government in the north of Spain. Bombings and assassinations characterize their tactics. Like the IRA in Northern Ireland, they seem to be semi-loved and semi-despised by the masses. But they are bent on violence in exchange for nothing less than full independence. Another of Spain's problems is the British, not only with regard to that perennial headache 'the Rock', but in relation to the new light industry of tourism.

A Pickfords van ploughed its way past me en route from Cadiz to Marbella. I imagined it to be transporting a retired English couple's belongings. It leaned heavily to one side under the weight of the tightly packed and securely harnessed furniture. It roared on past two boys on their motorbikes. These days mules have 50cc engines and carry less paniered gear. The fields that skirted the highway were full of bulls, not cows, bred for their blood not their milk. The hills, like the land, were scorched and stubbled, like a man's tufted chest too sparsely covered to be described as hairy. I turned from the coastal road and climbed inland, always seeing the shadowed, slightly misty outline of another hill beyond the one in front, an endless medley of mounds that teased me onward with the vain promise of eventual conquest. Every Spanish hill town seemed to have found the highest peak, each one arranged around a decayed castle and a well-kept church, creating a white-stone and red-roof shawl apparently to keep the top of the mountain warm while the lower slopes froze at night and burned in the day. Road signs announced rivers that had mysteriously left their beds by the time I reached them. It was as though I was on the trail of a kleptomaniac with a water fetish. I drove for sixty miles without seeing another car. Concrete blocks had been placed at the side of the road to prevent cars' driving over the edge. Occasionally there were a few missing, and a wreath and a couple of loose stones were piled on the spot, as though to avoid discussion of the obvious. I drove carefully into the cold shower of a shadow, then out again into the fire of the sun. *Sol y sombra*. Spanish sun and shade.

In Estapoña, a small tourist town on the western edge of the Costa del Sol, I met a waiter who had worked for fourteen years in the clubs of Manchester. We talked our way through the various ways of getting from England to Spain with a car. Then we switched to soccer and the great teams of the 1960s and 1970s. The names of Leeds United, Manchester United and Liverpool were repeated like a chorus. His wife's father was a director of Manchester United. I asked him why Laurie Cunningham, Britain's first black soccer star, never made it at Real Madrid. In return he asked me why another black soccer star, Luther Blisset, did not make it at AC Milan. I suggested, application? The climate? Lack of talent? The Italians, he explained, are prejudiced, hence Blisset's quick exit, while the Spanish just want to win at all costs.

Cunningham's problem was that he was injury-prone. Once he was injured he could never get back into the side, as his German replacement had already been imported. We then turned to the ritual drawing up of our all-time world eleven. By 3 a.m. the bar was deserted, we were drunk, he was in midfield, and I was playing up front with Pele and George Best. It seemed only fair that we should both be in the team.

Estapoña boasts the first nudist beach in Spain, a sad capitulation to the pressures of the tourist industry. The Spanish newsagents are packed with British newspapers and magazines. All along the Costa del Sol what were once pretty little villages have now, like Estapoña, been abused by commercial demands. I saw old Andalucians looking bewildered as men and women in skimpy beachwear cavorted past. Old styles and new clashed in the streets and in bars. The older Spanish women turned their heads away in shame and disgust as the semi-naked tourists lolled around what used to be peaceful and closed communities. As I drove along the coast road I could still see the odd fishing boat that had been hauled up on to the beach, but the illegally parked German camper vans and the illegally pitched student tents sported much higher profiles. This Costa del Sol main road was littered with what someone must have imagined to be attractive hoardings. For instance, 'full size snooker tables in our restaurant'.

As I neared Marbella the Barclays Bank and Lloyds Bank signs began to multiply. I was entering high investment and property dealing territory. In Marbella itself there were signs in Arabic. On shop fronts, apartment blocks, and hotels. The Arab-Hispanic bank dominated the main street. Marbella seemed to be for sale, and the dozens of 'disco-beach' clubs, and whitewashed apartment blocks looked like prison units. They stood pushed up against one another, like books in a cramped library, This vertical architectural nightmare made it exceedingly difficult to find the sea. Planning permission was either outmoded, or had never been practised in Marbella. In the midst of the boutiques, tennis parlours, and notices advertising 'English-speaking lawyers', I found a sign from a British building company which read, 'Wimpey says Welcome Home.'

Heading east along the Marbella–Malaga highway it was clear that Spain has attracted, whether in the form of permanent settlers or tourists, a vast number of British people. At least 100 of the British 'settlers' are, however, on a wanted list at Scotland Yard. As soon as an extradition treaty is worked out between London and Madrid, many of these 'settlers' will be quickly arranging their passage to Latin America. But the tourists will continue to come – or will they? Now nicknamed 'Costa de Crime', Spanish unemployment and increased drug-taking among the young have led to a growing spate of attacks by gangs of *tironeros*, which translated literally means 'those who pull the violence'. During six weeks in the summer of 1984 there were over 250 known attacks, including two deaths, in one Spanish tourist town alone. I continued to travel the Costa del Sol, but with caution. I also made a mental note that along this Marbella–Malaga stretch of highway, eighteen people had been killed during the previous ten weeks. It is a fast and dangerous stretch of road, swerving around the dead dogs being one of the many hazards. Spanish driving is, of course, the main problem.

As I drove on there seemed no end to the whitewashed chicken coops which posed as villas. 'Disco-pubs' begat more disco-pubs, and Italian meals were always available at 'Tony's Place', or an equivalent establishment. This Spanish sunstrip had all the thrill of the newly constructed housing estate. The buildings were a bit rickety, the cranes an eyesore, but nobody seemed to notice because it was new and offered a better and cleaner future with British exclusivity guaranteed, as, of course, locals cannot afford to buy. Many properties were advertised in sterling. Up above unfamiliar planes dotted the sky. They were nearly all charter flights with big orange suns painted on their tail-fins. In southern Spain, the pioneering zeal of El Cid (who has many restaurants named after him) is being fast replaced with the slothful and contemptuous lethargy of a Sid from England who has pubs and apartment blocks, hotels and golf-courses built in his honour.

In Torremolinos I found myself sitting out on the terrace of a bar whose two screens and external speakers were relaying a video tape of that week's *Top of the Pops*. All around there were young people in silly hats trying to chat each other up. Young girls together, young lads together, trying to pair off for a night, or perhaps even until the holiday finished. I listened to a black man with a white friend, both bare-chested and wearing trunks that were far too short. They were trying to impress two German girls, with obvious success. The girls both sported shocks of Bo Derek blonde hair under pushed-back sunglasses, loose vests and tight bikini bottoms. After the ritual staring, looking away, giggling, and the beer drinking contest, the black man started to tell racialist jokes. 'What do you call a black man who . . .?' 'Heard the one about Stevie Wonder in a tunnel?' The Irish jokes followed. I wondered what the German girls made of this. Did it reinforce their own prejudice? Or did it make them 'realize' that the guys were 'hip' and above all that racial shit?

Spanish men in black hats, white shirts with a red sash, and black pants, criss-crossed through the restaurants trying to sell half-dead flowers on the *señorita* circuit. In Torremolinos every street led to a precinct that was jammed with shops selling rubber rings, T-shirts, posters for non-existent bull-fights, cards, and suntan lotion. It appeared to be a whole town of nothing but precincts peopled by visitors, all competing to wear as little as possible. In Torremolinos the waiters must have at least a smattering of English, as the British make no effort to acquire any Spanish. To help the needy, many of the cafés and restaurants have gone to the trouble to provide pictures of their various plates of food, with the name of the dish captioned beneath in four different languages.

A short visit to Torremolinos left me with the feeling that the recent spate of murders and muggings may well have been inspired as much by anger at British behaviour as by criminality. The ugly clamour of football chanting, broken hotel rooms, furniture that is hurled into swimming pools, people pissing in the street, drunken brawling, neo-Fascist saluting, can be witnessed in the space of forty-eight hours. The British presence reminded me of similar behaviour on some of the Caribbean islands where little, if any, respect is shown for anything indigenously West Indian. Grossly overweight men, their fat spilling out and dribbling around their waists, oblivious to their Spanish surroundings, drank until they fell over.

It is only fair to point out that some Spaniards willingly aided this nonsense by displaying an alarming lack of taste in their frantic scramble for the English pound. 'Hotel El Gringo', 'Discotheek Voom Voom presents Saskia and Serge.' I found Frank's Bar next to the Rover's Return; then I stumbled across an empty plaza that was too shady for anyone to want to open a bar there. It had recently been renamed Plaza John Lennon. I grew to assume, from the number of signs, that the Spanish for rent-a-car was rent-a-car. And why could I only get the *Sun*, the *Star*, the *Daily Express* or the *Daily Mail*? As another Cliff Richard tape blared from the speakers hoping to attract the British in off the streets, I decided it was time to leave.

Malaga was the birthplace of Picasso. It has a huge and active port, and unlike the rest of the Costa del Sol it could flourish without the tourists. But, as the Central-Park-style carriages around the main park suggest, the holiday business helps. In the park itself teenagers posed with cigarettes, like extras in a 1950s film. In common with the rest of their countrymen, they are still thawing out from the chill of Franco's era. Smoking is chic, and contraceptives, illegal under Franco, are now available. I sat on a bench and listened as a woman read aloud from what sounded like a light nineteenth-century novel. She recited to her blind husband,

and as I looked at them I realized that they were both old enough to have lived through the Civil War. After eavesdropping for a time, I left the park and drifted into the evening *paseo* – the time of day when Spanish families come out to meet, walk, and talk in the streets before retiring. Then the peace was shattered by a plane approaching Malaga airport, which is located five kilometres outside the town. When the tourists disembark there they head west. By merely servicing the Costa del Sol, Malaga has ensured that when the bubble of cheap tourism bursts, she alone will survive this period of paganism intact.

Dinner at Jimmy's

Whenever I arrive at the tall iron gates separating James Baldwin from the outside world, my mind begins to wander. The gates remind me of prison bars. I wonder if Baldwin has been in prison, or whether this exile, his homosexuality, or his very spacious home are the different forms of imprisonment. My mind becomes supple, it feels strong and daring, and although the questions and thoughts Baldwin provokes are not always logical, I have always found that there is something positive and uplifting about his presence. Baldwin, unlike anybody else I have ever met, has this ability to kindle the imagination.

He is a much-photographed man so there is little I can add to the familiar image. Yes, he is small, but by no means diminutively so. His eyes bulge, but not as much as one might imagine. And, as the pictures often suggest, it is true that he is seldom without a cigarette. His face is highly distinctive, and he is recognized everywhere he goes. I have been in restaurants and bars with him in Britain, America and France, and in all three countries he has had to perform the task of shaking the quickly proffered hand or signing the book that has magically appeared as though from nowhere. No matter how full a restaurant might appear to be, Baldwin is always seated. His house is on the Provence 'Tourist Coach' itinerary, and much Kodak is burned by those who have heard of him but probably never read any of his books. Baldwin is a star; he knows and loves it.

That evening we stayed at home, ate dinner, drank an excessive amount of Johnnie Walker Black Label, and watched a bad disaster movie called *Airport 77*. The film had been dubbed into French. I laughed at the physical humour, Jimmy at the verbal. After thirty years on and off, though mostly on, as a resident, Baldwin's French is perfect. When the movie was over Jimmy switched off the television and began to talk about integrity, and the greatest crime an artist can commit, which is to abandon that gift in order to pursue money or honours or both. He was beginning a 'rap' I had heard from him before but this evening, Bernard Hassell, his personal assistant, was away in his gatehouse, and there were no other house guests. His tongue loosened by drink, his forehead streaked with tramlines of worry, Jimmy seemed to be finding words difficult to pin down. For such an eloquent talker, this suggested that I was now witnessing a Jimmy 'confession' rather than a Jimmy 'performance'.

He moved on with his chosen theme, saying that to give up the artistic gift for a woman seemed a preposterous act. Take Mailer, for instance, or Styron. Their problem was that while women, their various wives included, admired them, what they desperately craved was respect. As I knew neither Norman Mailer nor William Styron, their wives, nor their 'women', I was in no position to comment but Jimmy did not require any response. I was not an audience; as far as he was concerned I was merely present. He spoke on, and I tried to think of his own situation in relation to the other writers and artists on whose lives, misspent or otherwise, he passed judgement. I wondered how often he saw them, if he might be feeling just a little isolated, and worried about becoming a forgotten star.

Jimmy lives in St Paul de Vence, a hill village ten miles north of Nice. It is a colony which has attracted many of this century's foremost artists. Today its main residents are famous actors, Yves Montand, Donald Pleasence and Hardy Kruger among their number. The old walled city excludes cars. It is riddled with picturesque narrow, cobbled streets, so tightly squeezed that in places two pedestrians must come to some arrangement as to who shall pass first. The stone is sandblasted clean so there is little evidence of soot or grime.

St Paul de Vence has all the dramatic charm and aged glory of a Bavarian castle seen from the Rhine. The supposedly high-class art galleries, the 'chic' card and gift shops are of the expensive and exclusive variety. It is a discreet and civilized rip-off. In stark contrast to the cramped splendour of the walled St Paul de Vence, larger houses with sprawling estates fan out down the hillsides. Living outside the village walls means not only having a garden in which to roam, but also that you could easily afford to live inside the village walls if you wished – it is a voluntary exile. These are the two faces of a very expensive kingdom.

In the late 1960s St Paul de Vence accepted a new visitor. He was ill and had reached a low ebb in his life. The proprietress of a local restaurant-hotel looked after him. Having broken off from his first French sojourn to return to America and participate in the civil rights struggle, Baldwin had returned to France. He was an older and wiser man, but exceedingly distraught having endured the pain of living through the deaths of both Malcolm X and Martin Luther King Jr. The civil rights movement as he knew it had come to an end. In St Paul de Vence he found a house and an environment in which he could, in a sense, begin again. It would be the same struggle, but waged from a different standpoint.

His home is a child's paradise of ten acres. It is graced by three eighteenth-century properties: an outhouse, a gate-house, and the main villa itself. Jimmy lives and works in the basement of the main villa, in a two-roomed apartment he calls the torture chamber. The principal thoroughfare across his land is fringed with high rambling grass and a chain of different-coloured bulbs strung out between the trees. In the orchard there are lemons, olives, figs, bananas, pineapples, and pears. The land and property are enveloped by a high stone wall to ward off would-be trespassers. Bernard apart, there are no other black people resident in St Paul de Vence.

As I sat with Jimmy he continued to talk about respect and integrity, and about the old days in Paris when he, Richard

41

Wright and Chester Himes used to sit out on the Left Bank at the Café Tournan, or the Café Monaco. There was a tinge of nostalgia in his voice. I knew that he was currently involved in legal wranglings over his new book, *The Evidence of Things Not Seen*. It had started life as an award-winning essay for *Playboy* magazine, about the murder of twenty-eight young black males in Atlanta between 1979 and 1981. On delivery the book commissioned from the article had been rejected. For a writer of Baldwin's stature this was a terrible blow and had created a crisis of confidence, not so much in Jimmy himself, but in the way in which he felt others now perceived him. During his fifty-ninth year he had suffered a minor heart attack, and now had bronchial and tracheal problems. Every half-dozen sentences were punctuated by a high nasal whine, then a sharp, messy blowing of his nose into a large white handkerchief. The biblical, incantatory patter of his speech was peppered with the rhythms of age and illness. What was his legacy to be? Would his works be suddenly taken out of print on his death? He was sixty and not getting any younger. And there was yet more work to be done on *The Evidence of Things Not Seen*.

The following evening Jimmy pressed me to dine with him and his guest Miles Davis, who was playing at the Nice jazz festival. Only a few months before I had seen Davis at the Royal Festival Hall in London. His audiences now are often indistinguishable from those who would attend a Beethoven symphony or a Brahms concerto. They listened attentively with looks of rapturous homage etched across their faces. I had always wondered what Davis made of this, and whether, as Leroi Jones had once suggested, he really was blowing 'fuck you' down his trumpet, and also whether the Miles Davis of today was the same man who had played with Charlie Parker at Birdland. My head was swimming with questions to field to him, but I decided not to attend the dinner. I made some lame excuse, walked up the hill into the walled village, and felt miserable.

I sat alone and drank beer in the first bar that I came to,

pretending to read a book. When the manager of the bar switched on the television I began to watch the news intently. Then I felt embarrassed that somebody might ask me to comment on a particular item. As I understood only about 20 per cent of the chatter, I left the bar rather than risk appearing foolish. A little way up the hill I found a small terrace café where I sat discontentedly and ordered some food. I idly held the fork, and failed to notice as the food fell from it and splashed olive oil on to my new trousers. To compound my clumsiness, I accidentally knocked over my bottle of beer, and the Frenchman at the next table began to shout. I shrugged my shoulders. People were looking at me. I should have stayed at Jimmy's, I thought, but it was too late now.

I had left Jimmy's before Miles Davis arrived. The reasons for my departure may seem a trifle feeble now, but I felt them intensely at the time. Part of me desired, however naïvely, access to whatever conversation they might have on more equitable terms than my age and status would allow, but the more important reason lay in the heart of Jimmy's talk the previous evening.

I had never before noticed how lonely Jimmy was. His garrulity could always overwhelm any occasion, company, or atmosphere; he is a larger-than-life character. But that night his quiet conversation was so saturated with references to his past, to what other writers should have done, and to people that he knew I had never heard of, but whom he still felt compelled to talk about, that I realized that he needed to be alone with someone who could relate fully to all the nuances of his predicament, past, present, and future. 'When Sidney Poitier goes to the Cannes Film Festival he always calls by.' 'When Miles Davis comes to Nice, he stops by too.' A spiritual fix is a serious business, especially when they come as irregularly for Jimmy as they do these days. I would only have been in the way.

I overtipped the waitress. It was my way of apologizing for the chaos I had unwittingly caused on such a busy night for her. August 15 is a big holiday in France. As I began to stagger back down the hill, I passed hordes of people walking up it to witness the midnight fireworks display. The hill played havoc with the muscles on the back of my legs, but some fifty yards before I reached Jimmy's garden, I smelt the flowers. It was a warm, clear summer's night, and I stopped outside the huge iron gates. The lights were on, and in the distance I heard a laugh. A Renault roared past, its headlamps disappearing like two eyes closing in the darkness. Across the road four blue-suited gendarmes eyed me suspiciously. Two stood attentively, while the other two were perched on a Citroën bonnet. They all had guns on their hips, and all but one had a Gauloise cigarette in his mouth. They scowled in my direction – French policemen seldom smile. I heard another laugh from inside the house, then one of the perched policemen turned to the others and passed a comment. He twisted back round and stared again at me. *'Les nègres, ils s'amusent bien, n'est-ce pas?'* Perhaps he did not say that, and I simply imagined he did. Either way I did not care. I ambled on past the gates and down the hill. Up above the firework display began. Later, much later, I would sneak in unobserved and unheard. Like a naughty schoolboy, I slipped quietly into bed and listened to the old men's laughter until dawn broke.

A black European success

*In so far as truly interracial marriage is concerned, one can
legitimately wonder to what extent it may not represent for the
coloured spouse a kind of subjective consecration to wiping out
in himself and in his own mind the colour prejudice from which
he has suffered so long.*

Louis-T. Achille, *Rhythmes du Monde*, 1949

I saw only one other black man in Venice. He looked nothing
like Othello. His upper lip curled slightly upwards in a
manner that would make it difficult for him to grow a
moustache. Small and bespectacled, he carried a briefcase. I
was raised in Europe but Venice looked strangely distant and
eerie. A city of 117 islands glued together by 450 bridges. In
its heyday it was the New York of the Renaissance, control-
ling the whole of the Western world, dedicated to capitalism
and an unthinking exploitative trade. Today, its faded
imperial glory is celebrated by the thousands of tourists who
flock into the city all year round. But time is running out.
Venice is sinking, literally.

How did Othello live in this astonishing city? Sixteenth-
century Venetian society both enslaved the black and ridi-
culed the Jew. This black 'extravagant and wheeling stranger'
must have lived on a knife-edge. Out of this tension Shakespeare spun great drama. But the true nature of Othello's
psychological anguish is often missed in productions of the
play. We have been subjected to a procession of sun-blotched
Oliver Hardy lookalikes waddling across the English stage,
causing worry both to themselves and their audiences as to
whether or not the make-up will come off on the face of

Desdemona. I may be in danger of stating the obvious, but I shall state it anyhow. Othello was a black man. He was also a military man, a man of action, not a thinker. Like many soldiers he lacked intellectual acumen, psychological insight, and at times plain common sense. But then again, if he had possessed an abundance of these qualities he would have been sitting behind a desk in the Doge's Palace planning the war, rather than executing the campaign. However, it is not Othello's lack of a university degree that leads to his eventual demise, for there is another, more important factor at work.

Imagine this situation. A man is born of royal blood. You capture him, teach him another language – your language – mock his religion, teach him yours, make him dress in your clothes, make him realize quickly that in your society he can never be your equal. Then you discover that he is brilliant at soldiering, a natural leader of men, so you give a bit, and a bit more, until he becomes a general in your clothes, in your language, in your army. Then he goes too far and secretly woos and marries the daughter of one of your leading citizens. You are outraged, her father disowns her, but since there is a war on you tolerate the man. For the moment. You cannot expect a man with his history to behave rationally. And he does not. It is not a 'flaw' in the man, it is what you have made him into. Venice created the insupportable loss-leader, the most famous of all the black European successes. But the pressures placed upon him rendered his life a tragedy.

Before we meet Othello he has been called, barely within the space of thirty-five lines, 'an old black ram', 'a Barbary horse', and 'a lascivious Moor'. Othello's military reputation, already established as well earned and unchallengeable, is undermined by the bitter lack of respect for him as a man. This disrespect is related to the colour of his skin and the myths and fears it engenders. And his abusers, it should be noted, include a Venetian gentleman, a senator, and Othello's own ancient, Iago. Othello's position is tenuous to say the least. In his very first speech he subconsciously acknowledges the social pressure that he is under, by immediately making reference to his past services to the state.

> My services, which I have done the signiory,
> Shall out-tongue his complaints,

Then he makes reference to the thing that, as an ex-slave, he values above everything, his freedom.

> But that I love the gentle Desdemona,
> I would not my unhoused free condition
> Put into circumscription and confine
> For the sea's worth

The problems of justifying his ascent from slave to revered and contracted soldier 'in the service of the Venetian state' dominate his mind. He cannot help but be overwhelmingly aware that his origins are out of tune with his present position. And, naturally enough, the colour of his skin means that he cannot disguise this fact from others. In short, he feels constantly threatened, and is profoundly insecure.

Othello resorts to heroic posturing and powerful oratory to try and compensate for his lack of inner confidence. But at every turn he is reminded that he is working within the parameters of an authority he is not quite sure of, for unlike Cassio who is simply 'a foreigner', Othello is an alien, socially and culturally. Life for him is a game in which he does not know the rules. He describes his wooing of Desdemona in this manner. 'It was my hint to speak, such was the process;' And, 'Upon this hint I spake:'. What Othello really needed was a close friend who could help him figure out the complexities of Venetian society. Only then would he be able to relax a little. What Othello decided to do instead was get married.

Naturally enough Othello is cautious in his flirting, Desdemona having viewed him as something 'she feared to look on'. To the Venetian nobility he is a sorcerer, a sooty-bosomed man of proverbial black magic, as opposed to 'the wealthy curled darlings of our nation'. But Othello persists, knowing that marriage to her may entrench him securely in Venetian society, in a way that the transience of military achievement never could. Eventually he wins her hand and secretly marries her. And then he wins the approval of the nobility, who have to deliberate over whether Desdemona was won with love, or with a combination of witchcraft and aphrodisiacs. But their swift decision in his favour only comes about because they need Othello to go immediately to Cyprus and defeat the 'enemy Ottoman'. When a war is raging an 'unacceptable' marriage is of secondary import. And so Othello's love-plot succeeds, and Desdemona becomes inextricably tied in with his public life. Herein lie the seeds of disaster, for there is, in marriage to Desdemona, a new freedom, a security over and above a mere contractual position. As soon as the Venetian nobility says 'yes' to the marriage, Othello relaxes. The Duke's parting words to Desdemona's father are the final stamp on the seal of his approval. 'Your son-in-law is far more fair than black.' Othello has married into the society, the commonest form of acceptance. It is now that the tragedy commences. But it can only do so because it is precisely at this moment of 'triumph' that Othello begins to forget that he is black.

In Cyprus Othello is a revered leader. He is outside the hierarchical boundaries of Venice, he is married, and there is peace. His first speech on arrival in Cyprus betrays the dangers of his newfound tranquillity. 'My soul hath her contents so absolute,' he says, and goes on to state that he dotes in his own comforts. He leaves with Desdemona for the couch of luxury, an increasingly familiar exit. When Othello re-enters he is confident enough to use the Christianity he has assumed as a measure of 'their' Venetian superiority. He asks,

> *Are we turned Turks, and to ourselves do that*
> *Which heaven has forbid the Ottomites?*

However, balanced against this new confidence, there still exists an impulsive and insecure man who can best express himself in terms of physical violence, which is the last resort of the truly confident and socially secure man, the first refuge of the desperate.

> *Zounds, if I stir,*
> *Or do but lift this arm, the best of you*
> *Shall sink in my rebuke*

He wrongly dismisses his second-in-command, Cassio, then appoints the trusted Iago to that post. He thinks that he has found the friend he needs to help him in this foreign company. To those around him he asks militarily brisk and uncomplicated questions, and he demands sharp answers. It is when these questions and answers begin to relate to his white wife that Othello's world starts to fall apart.

In the security of Othello's 'For she had eyes and chose me' is gross insecurity. Their marriage had been founded on the unstable structure of mutual admiration.

> *She loved me for the dangers I had passed,*
> *And I loved her that she did pity them.*

When Iago begins to allude to the superior social status of Desdemona, Othello begins to display signs of losing the little control that he has, hence the epileptic fit. Iago invades Othello's 'tranquil mind', until Othello makes the final fatal mistake of beginning to question his own judgement. Why, asks Iago, did she not make a match 'Of her own clime, complexion, and degree'? Surely 'we may smell in such a will most rank'. Othello's response is again characterized by threats of anger and physical violence, 'I'll tear her all to pieces', but he is still not convinced. 'Villain, be sure thou prov'st my love a whore' are the words of a man who knows that he has totally misread the situation. But before he can reject her he needs evidence, and he gets it in the shape of a misplaced handkerchief. The flimsiness of the evidence only serves further to point up the tragedy of Othello's demise. 'Farewell the tranquil mind! Farewell content!' Having decided that Desdemona has been unfaithful to him, 'Chaos is come again.'

Othello kills her. His love for her is the love of a possession. She is a prize, a spoil of war, and he kills her rather than surrender her to the enemy, exacting a soldier's revenge. Having done so, when Emilia enters his bedchamber he denies the murder. 'You heard her say, herself, it was not I.' But then he acknowledges that it is useless. Instinctively he knew Desdemona to be 'true', but in order to submit to instinct one has to feel safe. Othello castigates himself for having reverted to the practice of a damned slave, but the truth is that even in marriage he only felt marginally more secure than he did as a bachelor. In his final speech Othello recognizes that he has lost everything. He dwells on his services to the state, but knows now that it is all going to count for nothing. 'No more of that.' Othello realizes that the only thing he can be sure of in Venetian society is that he is a black man. He had fallen for a white girl, married her, and tried to achieve equity in the society through her. Society wreaked a horrible vengeance on them both.

Othello's frame of mind can be summed up as that of the 'abandonment-neurotic'. The Martiniquan psychiatrist Frantz Fanon wrote of such a patient in the following way: 'The abandonment-neurotic demands proof. He is not satisfied with isolated statements. He has no confidence. Before he forms an objective relation, he exacts repeated proofs from his partner. The essence of his attitude is "not to love in order to avoid being abandoned".' Othello is inevitably abandoned, not by his wife, but by Venetian society. He assists in his own destruction, for without a peer group to reinforce his own sense of identity he is totally alone. He has to play by Venetian rules, and historically the dice are loaded against black men in the European arena. He needs allies, perhaps just someone he can turn to and ask, 'Listen, what the hell is going on with these people?' But he remains alone.

Othello was the Jackie Robinson of his day. He was a black first. The first black general, not in Verona or Padua, but in the major league, Venice. He fought his way up from slavery and into the mainstream of the European nightmare. His attempt to secure himself worked, but only as long as there was a war and he was needed. Othello relaxed, like the black man in the middle-class suburb who is suddenly surprised to see racist graffiti daubed on the side of his house. He thought he had escaped all that, but he never could. There is no evidence of Othello having any black friends, eating any African foods, speaking any language other than theirs. He makes no reference to any family. From what we are given it is clear that he denied, or at least did not cultivate his past. He relied upon the Venetian system, and ultimately he died a European death – suicide.

In the ghetto

*. . . the Jew must see that he is part of the history of Europe,
and will always be so considered by the descendant of the slave.
Always, that is, unless he himself is willing to prove that this
judgement is inadequate and unjust.*

James Baldwin, from an essay entitled, 'Negroes are
anti-Semitic because they're anti-white', 1969

The Venetian ghetto was the original ghetto, the model for
all others in the world – places characterized by deprivation
and persecution. Legally created in 1516, it further isolated
the Jews who had first come to Venice in 1373 to avoid
mainland persecution. It was windowless on its outside to cut
it off from the rest of the city. Jews were forced to wear a
special hat, they were not allowed to move in and out of the
ghetto after dark, and its iron gates were guarded by Christians. Today it is still a Jewish district, with its synagogue,
Jewish bakery and kosher shops, and a small Jewish museum.
As I wandered past the tall buildings that threw shadows
everywhere, with open shutters and washing hanging out,
the tiny streets were empty until I came to a large square. It
was speckled with benches and a clump of young trees. An
old man sat alone and concentrated hard, as though deter-
mined to wrestle on for a few more years. In the distance two
boys kicked a tennis ball back and forth. I watched them for a
while, then walked across to a memorial plaque inscribed in
three languages (French, English and Italian) and dedicated to
the two groups of Venetian Jews taken in 1943 and 1944 to
die in the concentration camps of the Holocaust.

One of the aspects of black America that I have never been

able to comprehend fully is the virulent anti-Semitism that seems to permeate much black thought. While still a student, I remember being surprised by Harold Cruse's words: 'The problem here is that the American Jew has a very thin skin, and believes that he is preternaturally free of all sin in his relationship with other peoples.' I was horrified by Louis Farrakhan's statement that the Jews faced 'God's ovens' if they continued to oppose him. But when I look again at Cruse's statement the word 'American' jumps out at me. Surely the Jew has not had to endure in America the persecution that has blighted 2000 years of his history in Europe? In fact, the American Jewish group has the highest per capita income ratio of any group in the United States – they have power. That an American black might respond with contempt to an American Jew who told him, 'I know what it means to be persecuted; I am a Jew', is easily understandable, particularly so when the tradition that is responsible for the European oppression of the Jew is a Judaeo-Christian one, the same one that continues to oppress black Americans. In Harlem, and most inner city areas of America, generation after generation of Jews have owned the shops, sold their goods to blacks, then locked up and left at the end of the day for more salubrious suburbs. I suppose what black Americans may be saying is, 'For 2000 years you might have been Europe's niggers, but now you're in America don't pretend you're not pleased to have discovered real ones. After all, one of your guys, Al Jolson by name, used to black up, mimic us offensively, and rake in millions. We never saw any of the cash.' Back in Europe things are not quite so straightforward.

For those on the right (and some in the centre and on the left too) the Jew is still Europe's nigger. I was brought up in a Europe that still shudders with guilt at mention of the Holocaust. Hundreds of books have been published, many films made, television programmes produced, thousands of articles written. The Nazi persecution of the Jews is taught at school, debated in colleges, and is a part of a European

53

education. As a child, in what seemed to me a hostile country, the Jews were the only minority group discussed with reference to exploitation and racialism, and for that reason, I naturally identified with them. At that time, I was staunchly indignant about everything from the Holocaust to the Soviet persecution of Jewry. The bloody excesses of colonialism, the pillage and rape of modern Africa, the transportation of 11 million black people to the Americas, and their subsequent bondage were not on the curriculum, and certainly not on the television screen. As a result I vicariously channelled a part of my hurt and frustration through the Jewish experience. Today, however, I find myself in agreement with the critic George Steiner in feeling that some of the policies of modern-day Israel, particularly with relation to South Africa, bring 'shame on the Jewish people'. But, as a black man living in Europe, I always remember the words of Frantz Fanon, who wrote in 1952 that, 'It was my philosophy professor, a native of the Antilles, who recalled the fact to me one day: "Whenever you hear anyone abuse the Jews, pay attention, because he is talking about you." ' And I always pay attention. Perhaps this explains why I have never been able to admire *The Merchant of Venice*. Even allowing for the historical times in which the play was first produced – when it was highly unlikely that the average Elizabethan knew what a Jew looked like, his prejudice being more ignorance than hostility – there is no denying that the play is anti-Semitic in its assumptions. For the present-day audience this is all the more disturbing given the evidence of recent European history.

The Venice in which the play is set was the hub of the world's financial empire. It existed simply to make a profit from financial deals. Buying goods cheaply and selling them at a higher price, rather than producing them. Jews were tolerated as usurers, needed and patronized by society but shamefully castigated as outcasts in a manner similar to that in which modern society sneers at, and thereby attempts to reduce, the prostitute. Antonio, the hero of the play, spits on

54

Shylock's coat, then spits in his beard, and kicks him like a dog. Shylock has always been my hero. He makes it uncompromisingly clear that he wants nothing to do with Christians beyond his business. 'I will buy with you, sell with you, talk with you, and so following; but I will not eat with you, drink with you, nor pray with you.' He is advocating separatism and, as many black Americans will testify, there is a time when such a debate is necessary. Shylock further refuses to charge interest on his loan to Antonio, who is absolutely sure that his ships will arrive in time to repay the debt. Shylock is doing the man a favour, while showing him where the power lies. And finally, in the trial scene, amid all the high-flown self-righteousness about 'the quality of mercy', is it not Shylock who, in Othello's city where blackness is equitable with devil-worship, points out to the Christian Venetians that,

> You have among you many a purchas'd slave
> Which, like your asses and your dogs and mules,
> You use in abject and in slavish parts.

In her book, *Out of Africa*, Karen Blixen describes how she 'explained' *The Merchant of Venice* to one of her houseboys, Farah, because 'Farah, like all people of African blood, liked to hear a story told . . .' But to Blixen's dismay Farah's sympathy was with Shylock. The Jew's insistence in going ahead and taking his pound of flesh, the moment in the play when we are theoretically supposed to lose our sympathy with Shylock, produced no such response in Farah. ' "Look, Memsahib," he said, "he could have taken small bits, very small. He could have done that man a lot of harm, even a long time before he had got that one pound of his flesh." ' Blixen was outraged, but Farah continued to think it 'a great pity' that Shylock gave up his pound of flesh. I think that most black Americans, despite anti-Semitic statements, would have some understanding of Farah's position, and by extension, that of Shylock.

Autumn in Paris

Cocteau became irritated with Paris – 'that city which talks about itself the whole time'. Is Europe any different? And that super-European monstrosity, North America? Chatter, chatter: liberty, equality, fraternity, love, honour, patriotism, and what have you. All this did not prevent us from making anti-racial speeches about dirty niggers, dirty Jews, and dirty Arabs.

Jean-Paul Sartre, Introduction to Frantz Fanon's
The Wretched of the Earth, 1961

He said the Negroes knew how they stood among the Americans, but the French were hypocrites. They had a whole lot of say, which had nothing to do with reality.

Claude McKay, *Banjo*, 1929

In the rain Paris looks suspiciously like London. This is one of the reasons I dislike France. It reminds me of Britain, the sun making its sad attempt to get there for an hour or so each day. France is proud, modern, aloof and full of self-importance. Impressive TGV trains scream across the country at 160 m.p.h. It boasts Concorde, vast nuclear potential and a space programme.

As the train edged its way forward and began to choose a platform, the first sight that arrested my attention was a sign sprayed up on the wall of a Parisian house. I wondered on which side I would have to disembark, and looking up I read the words, '*L'Invasion nègre*'. I assumed that it did not refer to myself alone. A slow persistent drizzle cast a mournful aspect over both the sky and my mood: I arrived in this grey city not having seen rain for six months. Between the crowd of tall buildings, cars swished through puddles with their sidelights on, and the noise and aggression outside the Gare de Lyon was overpowering. A West Indian helped me with my bags. An Asian sold me a copy of *Pariscope*, the local guide to theatre and films, and a Senegalese tried to sell me some dope. In *Pariscope* I read that a local black theatre company was performing in a large and prestigious theatre. In another magazine I read an article condemning the group for allowing themselves to be used as 'token blacks'. In McDonald's I escaped from the insistent clamour of the streets and was served by a youth with a Walkman clamped on to his head. Paris, France. The lines outside the cinema suggested that most would rather be in Paris, Texas. Where was the romance?

After a few days I discovered what I had always suspected, that I could not possibly live in Paris. All that would happen was I would learn a new language with which to tackle old problems. The racialist signs multiplied each day, and 'Arabs pick pockets' seemed to be a favourite. One evening the waiter in a cheap Pigalle Indian restaurant whispered to tell me that we were brothers, and that the French were the worst kind of white people. I asked him if he had ever been to Britain. He said, 'No.' I offered up a lame comparison of the British and the French, which concluded in my unwitting defence of the French against such blanket condemnation. He looked horrified and quickly found somebody else to attend as I finished my meal in silence.

The official French categories for black people are complex to grasp. A journalist on *Libération*, the newspaper that middle-class parents read when they want to know what their rebellious children are thinking, attempted to guide me through this ethnological maze. He prefaced his talk with the line, 'without getting into apartheid I will try to explain', and went on to step straight into apartheid. It was not necessarily his fault. As a journalist he was a paid inventor of labels and categories, and the shrewd hypocrisy of French society had provided him with a skilled teacher. He identified the West Indians, who came principally from Martinique and

Guadeloupe, as the most privileged of the blacks. They generally arrived in France already furnished with jobs in the post office, transport or construction. Both Martinique and Guadeloupe are *départements* of France, they are not colonies but fully integrated parts of metropolitan France, in the same way that Hawaii is related to the United States. The 4000-mile transatlantic flight from Paris to either island is an internal one. I remember my initial shock on the short flight from Barbados to Martinique, when the stewardess passed around the disembarkation forms for passport control and I read question nine: Proposed length of stay in France? Both Martinique and Guadeloupe send deputies to the French Assembly, and theoretically at least, West Indians in France suffer no disadvantages for they are French. I was informed that the real problem with the islands was not the pro-independence lobby, who have been waging a bombing campaign for some time, but the regulation of large numbers of white French people who want to leave metropolitan France to go and live there. According to my journalist friend, the islands were 'apparently very beautiful'.

He then went on to talk about 'the Africans'. Most of them were from Senegal, Mali and Mauritania, and those from the Congo, which became Bokassa's Republic, are able to claim status as political exiles. He was sure that most of these 'Africans' were here illegally, and they showed no sign of leaving. I suggested drought and poverty as possible reasons for their French exile, two facts of African life that seem in danger of becoming permanent. It was a point of view he conceded before swiftly pressing on with his definition of the third category, the 'North Africans'. After some probing I came to understand that North African was a euphemism for Arab. This category embraced the people of Tunisia, Morocco, and Algeria. Like the Africans, these North Africans were deemed mainly 'illegals' who displayed no intention of vacating the premises, despite the Government's offer of 10,000 francs compensation to any 'migrant' who wished to 'go home'.

What my informant omitted to mention was that there are, in total, 4 million immigrants in France. Of these only 2 million are black, the rest are European, primarily Spaniards or Portuguese. In Paris one person in five is an outsider, a foreigner of some kind, and despite the much vaunted right-wing slogan, '2 million immigrants [for which you read 'black immigrants'] – 2 million unemployed', the French economy would collapse without black people. Without them the price of labour would double overnight, assuming that the whites would consider doing the jobs and enduring the conditions under which the blacks have to toil. In an attempt to try and unravel this potpourri of facts and figures, I went to the Ministry of Industry where I met with the Socialist Government spokesman on affairs to do with North Africans.

His secretary was a Martiniquan. She had the look of a woman who has seen many politicians come and go over the years. The spokesman's name was typed on a piece of card and slotted into a holder on the door. His office was comfortable and well lit. After formal introductions we sat down. He was middle-aged and studious. I imagined him as a senior lecturer in literature or another branch of the humanities. In this environment he seemed uneasy, in his anxious attempt to cultivate an air of self-importance and to appear both liberal and tough. His suit was sharply creased, his tie freshly knotted, and his nails recently manicured. The smartness of his attire made me wonder if he was going to the theatre after work, before returning to the leafy exclusivity of the 8th or 16th *arrondissements*.

He immediately informed me that he was an 'expert' on North African 'affairs' – travelling there regularly, mainly to visit Algeria. Then he raised the telephone to summon some unrequested statistics. There were 189,000 Tunisians in France, 800,000 Algerians, 138,000 French-speaking black Africans (including Madagascans), and 431,000 Moroccans. Was I aware that the Air France Paris–Algeria route flew at 95 per cent capacity all year round? He claimed that this was the highest capacity rating in the world for any international route. I asked him if the route was a monopoly. He asked me if I was a student. For the second time I told him that I was a writer. As I asked if he spoke Arabic, the phone rang. The perfect timing of the interruption, convinced me that he had a secret bell fitted behind his desk. When he put the phone down he asked me which college I was attending. Seeing no way out of this conversational impasse, I returned to my earlier question and asked if he spoke Arabic. He leant back in his chair, knitted his fingers together, popped them into an arch and asked me if I was not aware that North Africans spoke French as well. I smiled. France was glad to have black people, he said, because of the trade they bring. Food, hair-dressing, and shirts, were offered as examples. 'Shirts?' I asked. Yes, of course, shirts. I changed my tack. Did he not feel that the French harassment of black Britons trying to enter France, an EEC partner, on seventy-two-hour pass-ports was a disgrace? What harassment? I reminded him that it had so embarrassed his Government that they had now scrapped the long-established seventy-two-hour passport system altogether. Ah, well, it was outmoded anyhow, he said. I realized that this talk could not be saved, but I tried one final question. Given the resurgence of Fascist feeling, exemplified by the rise of the National Front, how did his Government go about both combating neo-Nazi propaganda and mollifying the fears of the black population? He smiled. 'The National Front', he maintained, 'are not to be taken too seriously.'

In the 1984 elections for the European Parliament, the National Front took 11 per cent of the French national vote (which represents 2 million voters). They have ten seats in the Strasbourg Assembly. They are led by Jean-Marie le Pen, a man singled out in police reports as being responsible for the electric shock torture of an Algerian prisoner in the late 1950s, and convicted by the police of compiling and dis-tributing a record of Nazi war songs. He describes multi-racialism as 'a way of disguising the conquest of Europe by the Third World', and is often quoted as having said 'I'm not an anti-Semite. On the other hand I don't feel obliged to like Madame Veil, Chagall's paintings or Mahler's music.' During the previous Euro-elections (1979) the National Front had been conspicuous for disrupting meetings led by Simone Veil (an Auschwitz survivor, and Giscard's Minister of Health). They threw eggs at her and called her 'a dirty Jew'.

As Mitterrand's Socialist Government becomes increasingly unpopular, and the centre right begins to splinter into inter-factional disarray, the National Front is gradually filling a gap in French politics. Before the 1986 parliamentary elections, an opinion poll showed that 70 per cent of the electorate believed that immigration was the dominant factor in the elections. The main recruiting drive of the National Front is among the under-twenty-fives, which especially worries the left for it takes votes from their main recruiting area – idealistic youth. The strength of the Fascist movement, however, is provided by the middle-class shopkeeper – the grocer who likes uniforms and giving orders. These days their main rallying cry centres on the 'African scourge'. They make much of the fact that they are not against the West Indians. When asked how they knew the difference between the various ethnic groups, a spokesman replied that the Senegalese were the tall ones who tried to sell you things, and the Malians were the even taller ones who cleaned the streets.

Outside the Georges Pompidou Centre I met a Nigerian who, after two minutes of polite conversation broke into a performance of his stand-up comic routine. He soon attracted a sizeable crowd, and he can best be described as a Nigerian Richard Pryor. But, unlike Pryor, he had only one target to abuse – the French. I wandered off toward the garishly lavish Les Halles complex, where some Africans were break-dancing. One man began to limbo, and of all the performers it was he who was making the money. In the overcrowded and rat-infested 19th and 20th *arrondissements* where most black immigrants live, life cannot be much fun.

By contrast, the lights and glitter of central Paris are irresistible. Many of the city centre Métro stations house illicit dealers. Drugs are peddled, activists hand out leaflets, performers perform. There is little to distinguish these twilight scenes from those in any large capital, except that most of the players in this drama are black. What surprised me was the participants' startling dress sense, with their zoot-suits, bowties, Burberry coats, cravats, Gucci shoes, and Oxford bags – there seemed to be enormous peer group pressure to 'dress'. This, I was led to believe by my journalist friend, distinguished young Africans from other black people in France. They were, of course, much more 'bitter' than the West Indians, but much smarter. None of those awful dreadlocks.

I took the Métro out to the Belleville district of Paris, which was like riding the train up into Harlem. The white passengers began to disappear as the train drew nearer to the black area showing demographic apartheid in action. When I noticed the afro hair shops on the Métro platform, and record shops with names like Afridisc, I knew I had arrived. The cinemas of the Belleville area are full of Kung Fu and sex films. The films are pure distillations of sex and violence, offering instant gratification at the expense of narrative, plot and character. The district bustled with fruit markets and fully gowned Arabs. Water gushed from a burst mains pipe, and Arabs and blacks stooped together in the gutter to wash rags or cutlery, as though a small village stream ran below the surface of floating debris. Police cars screamed past, their unnecessary noise anticipating trouble. Pasty white prostitutes sat on benches, leaned up against cars, or drifted in front of sidewalk bars hoping somebody might fall out and into their arms for the evening. The women's bright clothes attracted clinging dirt and grime. In Belleville most Arabs wrapped loud tassled scarves around their necks, which looked like turbans that had slipped from their heads.

I noticed the Jewish bakeries, the Star of David painted on the windows as though defying the dangers of the anti-Semitic brick. Nestled next to these bakeries were the

Franco-Tunisian shops, the Halal butchers and the *patisseries orientales*, with Arabic script decorating the windows. Here Jew and Arab exist side by side aware of a common enemy. In the streets Christian Africans sported tribal scars, and mixed with Muslim Africans wearing tribal veils, while everybody mixed with the French who looked on with tribal hostility.

La Goûtte d'Or ('the golden drop') is perhaps the most notorious of the Parisian Arab quarters. At one time the police used to patrol the roads that led into this tightly knit ghetto. They still do so today, but unofficially. The brothels are distinguished by the length of the queues outside them, often containing forty or fifty men. Life for a prostitute in La Goûtte d'Or is still hard, but the main business of the sector is now commerce. It has the atmosphere of the Kasbah, as men stand in large groups selling perhaps a pair of pants, draped over an arm, or belts, rows of them dangling like snakes from an iron bar. Clothes are the biggest business, particularly second- or even third-hand overcoats to fight off the European winter. An individual holding a neatly wrapped skirt and two combs rapidly becomes a shop in this human sea of free enterprise. It is a mobile market that visibly expands and contracts depending upon supply and demand. But, the uniqueness of this area is under threat. The Parisian mayor, Jacques Chirac, has actively begun a policy of urban redevelopment, which means getting the blacks and Arabs out. As the people of Harlem are learning, inner city property is valuable.

I stood on the Métro platform waiting to leave the district, and watched a young black man as he lurched across the tracks, hip-hopping over the iron rails. He grabbed my arm and told me incredulously that he had been pickpocketed by whites. Then he realized that I spoke English. 'I am a black man,' he said. This was all the English he knew. 'I am a black man.' Then he added, '*Je suis un petit bois*' as an afterthought.

France, like Britain, combines racialism with an admiration for semi-chic black fashions in music – reggae, jazz, salsa, hi-life, soca, and soul. Black style, dance and food are popular, and singers from Eartha Kitt to King Sunny Ade to Nina Simone are best sellers. But racialism appears to be more widespread than at any time since the Algerian war of 1954–62. Blacks and Arabs are being shot almost weekly by the National Front and other neo-Fascist groups. Meanwhile, posturing aside, the French Government seems to be adopting the same ostrich-like position on the domestic front that they have cultivated on the foreign. In New Caledonia the Kanak people are pushing the French to the brink of another Algerian war in order to secure their independence. The French whites, the Caldoches, have been settled there for approximately 140 years, and constitute 36 per cent of the population, but own 70 per cent of the land. The Kanaks will not back down, nor will the blacks and Arabs in metropolitan France. But, at the moment, their response to French hostility has been surprisingly meek. There has been little evidence of the riots and aggression that have characterized the black British response.

The roots of French racialism lay in the classifications I had been offered by the *Libération* journalist on the commencement of my Parisian sojourn. More than any other European colonial power, France exported a culture that aimed to embrace blacks. They tried to make West Indians in particular but also Africans feel that they had a shared history, and they could have equality in Frenchness if in nothing else. This was helped by de Gaulle's famous wartime speech in Brazzaville, which forged romantic links between black Africa and Paris, and by the much-flouted fact that Le Clerc came to France's rescue at the end of the Second World War using African troops. Today, however, by careful nurturing of the French West Indies, and lack of action in responding to the grievances of the Arabs, the French have managed to split the black community. The Arabs are ghetto-ized, have few political rights, in the main hold foreign passports, and are almost universally viewed as a 'problem'. The black Africans are encouraged only as contract workers to be herded into hostels known as *foyers*, and they see little but these vermin-infested barracks and the factory floor where they toil. Those who arrived illegally, or who have managed to escape the *foyer* existence, roam the streets or pick up whatever work they can. In France they have no political rights, and what political energies they do expend refer back to their countries of origin. When asked about the West Indians the average Frenchman is happy to tell you that they have no problems, except racialism of course.

The French game is both clever and hypocritical, but it will only work as long as the Arabs, in particular, are a first generation. When their French children begin to demand their rights, together with the disillusioned West Indian youth and the children of the African, France may begin to experience the problems of inner city rioting that Britain has already had to come to terms with. It was interesting to note that during the Handsworth disturbances in Birmingham in 1985, the British Government and media were quick to try and drive a wedge between the black and Asian communities. Headlines such as, 'Why blacks hate Asians' became commonplace. France and Britain share many characteristics, but in this instance the French have transferred the colonial technique of divide and rule into the domestic arena, and perfected it almost to the point of a fine art. British racists have much to learn from the French.

Anne Frank's Amsterdam

> 'Then they will find Anne's diary,' added Daddy. 'Burn it
> then,' suggested the most terrified member of the party. This,
> and when the police rattled the cupboard door were my worst
> moments. 'Not my diary, if my diary goes, I go with it!' But
> luckily Daddy didn't answer.
>
> from *The Diary of Anne Frank*

I was about fifteen when Amsterdam first began to fascinate
me. There was a programme on television, part of the *World
at War* series, which dealt with the Nazi occupation of Holland and the subsequent rounding up of the Jews. Even in
black and white the broad boulevards, the little hump-backed
bridges, and the canals seemed attractive, and stood out in
contrast to the grey concrete council estate where I lived. It
was not just the aesthetic delights of the city that attracted
me. There was a deeper, more troubling aspect to my fasci-
nation which related directly to the Jews. One thing I could
not understand about the programme was why, when
instructed to wear the yellow Star of David on their clothes,
the Jews complied. They looked just like any other white
people to me, so who would know that they were different?
As the programme progressed my sense of bemused fasci-
nation disappeared and was supplanted by my first mature
feelings of outrage and fear. These yellow stars were marking
them out for Bergen-Belsen and Auschwitz. I watched the
library footage of the camps and realized both the enormity
of the crime that was being perpetrated, and the pre-
cariousness of my own position in Europe. The many adolescent thoughts that worried my head can be reduced to one

66

line: 'If white people could do that to white people, then what the hell would they do to me?'

After that programme I wrote my first piece of fiction. A short story about a fifteen-year-old Jewish boy in Amsterdam who argues with his parents because he does not want to wear the yellow Star of David. He is just like everyone else, he says, but his parents insist. Eventually there comes the knock on the door and his family are taken to the cattletrucks for 'resettlement'. En route the boy somehow manages to jump from the wagon, but in doing so he bangs his head. He lies bleeding by the railway embankment and it is only the sunlight shining on his yellow star that attracts a kindly farmer's attention. The boy is taken to the farmhouse and saved. My English literature teacher took this essay from me 'for publication', and that was the last I saw of it.

Amsterdam is a city of stark contrasts. The pleasantness of the architecture, the warm cosmopolitan nature of the people, the plethora of bookshops and sidewalk cafés is immediately attractive. A longer look at the city reveals that drugs and pornography are becoming increasingly intrusive.

Prostitutes sat in windows like goods on display, and the sallow-faced addicts slunk around the streets needing £90-worth of drugs just to get through to the next day. They moved like lean wolfhounds, with pock-marked skin and sunken cheeks, their jackets falling from their rounded shoulders, and broken shoes flapping loudly.

'Liberal' is the word most commonly coupled to the word 'Dutch', and it is certainly true that Amsterdam lacks the hard-nosed arrogance of Paris or London, but the lifestyles of Dutch black people, West Indians from Aruba, Curaçao or Surinam, Asians from Indonesia, made me immediately question the appropriateness of the label 'liberal'. A disproportionately high number of these black people were either in the windows selling their bodies, or drug addicts in the streets. I began to think that 'liberal' meant not tackling drugs and pornography; that being the case, it might also mean not tackling racism. After all, it should not be forgotten that the Dutch, despite having a brave and active resistance movement, also collaborated more fully with the Nazis than any other occupied territory: 23,000 of them volunteered for the SS.

The Anne Frank House is situated in the old part of Amsterdam. It is a tall, narrow, four-storey house overlooking a canal. In 1940 Anne's father, Otto, established his herbs and spices wholesale business in this house. He had left the family's native Germany in 1933 with his wife and two young daughters shortly after Hitler became Chancellor and initiated a boycott of Jewish businesses. In 1942, when it became clear that the Jews of Holland were going to fall victim to the German occupation, Otto Frank turned the annexe at the back of his building into a hiding place for his family and one of his employees. For just over two months Anne wrote her diary, depicting her inner fears about the occupation, her future life, her Jewishness, and her burgeoning sexuality. Her clarity of expression, her humility and courage make it one of the most important books of the century.

A black Dutch woman issued me with my ticket as I entered the Anne Frank House. A white colleague kissed her a morning greeting. I felt slightly embarrassed that I had even noticed this. Before I went round the house, I tried to think of what I knew about anti-Semitic thought. I knew that it had permeated the Roman Empire, that Christians had passed laws which made it impossible, or at best difficult, for Jews to mix. Jews became the victims of theft, repression, extermination and exile, and as Christianity spread so did anti-Semitic feeling. In Christian eyes the Jews were always going to have to atone for the death of Christ. After 1500, Protestantism became a little easier on the Jews and they came to settle in more northern European countries, such as Holland, until Martin Luther eventually adopted an anti-Semitic point of view. Theories were propagated, all of them supposedly serious, to try and justify Jewish inferiority. They included the 'fact' that Jews were going to take over the world, that Jews have bigger backsides, differently sized and shaped skulls, bigger noses, a greater propensity towards crime, and do not like to mix. Four decades into the twentieth century, in the age of Marx, Freud and Einstein, the inferiority of the Jew was still a generally accepted European assumption.

Walking round the annexe in which Anne Frank and her family secreted themselves, I was torn between feelings of anger and great despair. On a door the heights of Anne and her sister Margot are clearly marked. They were tall and still growing. The movie stars on the posters in Anne's bedroom include Norma Shearer, Deanna Durbin, Rudy Vallee, Sonja Henie, Greta Garbo, Ray Milland and Ginger Rogers, and are placed beside pictures of Princesses Elizabeth and Margaret Rose of York. In another part of the house there is an exhibition of family artefacts. Two strips of photographs from a machine in Aachen, taken in 1933–34, show a four- or five-year-old Anne with her sister and mother. They were just a normal family. I could not look any more. Then American voices began to cackle in my ears. A tourist party had arrived and I heard laughter punctuated by the aimless clicking of cameras. 'Her father wrote the book, didn't he?' someone said. 'I bet there's some shamefaced Germans, ain't there,' observed another. 'She died at the age of sixteen,' said another voice. 'She didn't die. They killed her.' At this point I moved away.

The final room in the Anne Frank House is dedicated to documenting Fascism in twentieth-century Europe. A photograph of a large banner during a 1924 Berlin demonstration caught my eye. The text on the banner read: '500,000 unemployed. 400,000 Jews. Solution very simple. National Socialism.' Behind the banner somebody held aloft an ugly caricature of a Jew. The swastika-armbanded men looked respectable in white shirts and ties. I have seen banners carrying such messages in London, but for 'Jew' read 'black'. Very little seems to have changed in the heart of Europe. To the side of this photograph was one of young German children being made to run their hands over the 'misshapen', 'big-lipped, bumpy-headed skull' of a Negro. Then they were introduced to the smooth-edged, classically shaped head of an Aryan.

Unemployment and the world economic crisis are nourishing this new European Fascism. There are seventy-four right-wing groups in West Germany with over 2,000 full-time members. These groups are anxious for the Eastern and Western parts of their country to be unified. In Holland, the Dutch Centrum Party present themselves as a decent anti-immigration movement who are simply worried about the 'Islamization' of Dutch cities. They recently tried to persuade the Dutch Parliament, where they have two members, to legitimize 'violence against minorities – in self-defence'. In the local elections of May 1984, a policeman was chosen to stand for the Centrum Party in a district of Rotterdam. The European industrial boom of the 1950s and 1960s is over, and whether 'guest-worker' or 'colonial migrant' the facts are clear. Non-Europeans are not wanted. In many ways the black man, while not replacing the Jew as an object of abuse, is more visible, and an equally vulnerable target for Fascist propaganda. In the Europe of the 1980s racist graffiti continue to smear synagogues, but are now also daubed on mosques. Arson is a growth industry, and racialism, both official and unofficial, is rampant. In West Germany it is a crime to scrawl '*Judenraus*', but not '*Turkenraus*'. Europe is in danger of swaddling herself in a familiar hypocrisy.

Holland is a very cosmopolitan society. Out of a population of 14 million, there are 180,000 from Surinam, 100,000 from Morocco, 150,000 from Turkey, 35,000 from Aruba and Curaçao, and 35,000 Moluccans. On a walk down any main shopping street in Amsterdam, Rotterdam or The Hague, windows display American afro hair products. Rastafarians mix freely in this society, their music is universally loved, and East Indian restaurants are often the most frequented. All this might give the impression of a swinging multi-racial country, but since the killing of a Dutch West

70

Indian in 1982 there has been a loss of innocence. I spoke with a young social worker whose family originated from Surinam. He commended the Anne Frank House highly, for among its other functions it supplies 2,500 Dutch schools with anti-racist materials. When I asked him about the current state of race relations he simply laughed, and then asked me what I had expected to find. 'I don't know,' I said. 'I suppose I expected it to be better than most places in Europe.' He slapped me on the back and laughed again. 'That's it, that's our problem. It's difficult to believe that the liberal Dutch could have a racist element in their society, isn't it?' I shrugged my shoulders. 'Well, they do,' he said. 'Not as much as some places, but it exists.'

I wandered back to the Anne Frank House but it was closed. Back at my hotel I picked up the *Diary* and began to re-read it. On Wednesday, 24 June 1942, the thirteen-year-old Anne wrote: 'It is not the Dutch people's fault that we are having such a miserable time.' On Tuesday, 11 April 1944, the fourteen-year-old Anne wrote: 'I love the Dutch, I love this country, I love the language and want to work here. And even if I have to write to the Queen myself, I will not give up until I have reached my goal.' Six weeks later, on Monday, 22 May, she was beginning to have her doubts.

> Quite honestly, I can't understand that the Dutch, who are such a good, honest, upright people, should judge us like this, we, the most oppressed, the unhappiest, perhaps the most pitiful of all peoples in the whole world. I hope one thing only, and that is that this hatred of the Jews will be a passing thing, that the Dutch will show what they are after all, and that they will never falter and lose their sense of right. For anti-Semitism is unjust!

Ten months later, the fifteen-year-old Anne Frank, her hiding place betrayed to the Nazis by Dutch collaborators, died in the concentration camp of Bergen-Belsen.

History is to blame

In the gutter lies the black man, dead,
      And where the oil flows blackest, the street runs red,
And there was He who was born and came to be,
      But lived and died without liberty.

                                    Bobby Sands, 1954–1981

At Heathrow the security was extensive. I arrived at Belfast airport somewhat surprised to find that I was still in Britain. East Germany or the Soviet Union would have been a more explicable destination after the thorough searches we had all endured. While the bags were being unloaded I went to find a telephone. They were the old-style pay telephones, where you break your thumb trying to push the money in, then wait for the machine-gunning of the pips before, usually, being cut off. At the furthest-flung outpost of a nation, technological advancements were obviously slow to arrive. I took up a place beside the still empty baggage conveyor. A three-year-old boy, his young cheeks red with cold, hid behind his father to peer fearfully up at me. Was it some article of my clothing that frightened him, or my face? The child's curiosity made me feel defenceless, a sharp stare being an uncharitable riposte to one so young, a smile and a wink liable to reduce him to tears.

Outside the terminal I found a taxi that deftly negotiated its way through the various security barriers, which meant that the airport could be sealed off at a moment's notice. As we sped towards Belfast I noticed the names of the towns on roadside signposts. Portadown, Newry, Armagh, Cookstown, Antrim, places that I had heard about on the news since I was eleven years old. The pretty pocket-sized fields, the small villages that we passed through, the charming rusticity of the countryside seemed at odds with the presence of British army patrols and the heavily armed Royal Ulster Constabulary who waited by the roadside with sternly erect rifles protruding from their armoured vehicles. Once in Belfast the taxi driver left me a hundred yards from the hotel. To drive into the car park would have meant his taxi having to be searched, and this could have taken anything up to half an hour. After sixteen years of 'Troubles' the driver still seemed irritated by this fact of Belfast life.

He set me down and I negotiated a security check, then walked across the car park. The doors to the hotel were of sliding glass, and I waited for them to open automatically as I approached. After signalling from inside, I realized that I would have to position myself so that the receptionist at the desk could see me. The idea is that if you don't appear to be a security threat, she presses a buzzer that releases the door. I passed. As I signed the register I enquired about the security. 'Well, we've been bombed a few times,' she said casually, as though replying to a question about the weather. 'And how long will you be staying with us, Mr Phillips?' I was no longer sure.

Belfast shopping centre is recognizably British. In the rain the people went about their business, heads bowed, shuffling from one shop window to another, one precinct to another, but of course there was one huge difference. Security, in the shape of the 'cage', a high fence that encircles the whole of the city centre. The Royal Ulster Constabulary, clad in bullet-proof vests, their guns holstered but clearly ready to be used, frisk both persons and packages on entry and exit. Vehicles, except those to be used for trade, are forbidden to enter the 'cage'. It is a shocking and frightening sight, one which finally drives home the point that Belfast is a war zone. The hurried, unconcerned looks on the faces of the shoppers seemed to me indicative of a people who have come to terms not with eventual victory, whatever that might

73

mean, but the horror of a permanent struggle.

The Troubles did not begin in 1969. Then, a temporary peace ended. Over 800 years of Anglo-Irish conflict has finally been reduced to a struggle for control of six of the eight counties of Ulster. The province is heavily dependent on mainland Britain, taking from the Treasury £1.5 billion more than it sends back in taxes. It is now peopled by a generation who remember no past free from civil strife and conflict. The army, largely made up of English youths, patrol the streets defending a cause they do not understand, full of antagonism towards a people they do not want to understand. Britain has effectively isolated its most durable and bloody problem to a place where Westminster can neither hear nor see it. It is all too easy to live in mainland Britain and switch off completely from the tragedy of what is happening in Ulster. The received wisdom of the media runs as follows: the IRA are murdering bastards, the Loyalists just chaps fighting for their right to remain in the land of their birth but who sometimes go a little too far. It is not a particularly sophisticated analysis of a crisis that has resulted in well over 2,000 deaths, and appears even more crude by comparison to the theory that propels the IRA. Its members feel that the use of random violence will infect society with such fear that paralysis will be induced, democracy come under scrutiny, and that as a result of this charged atmosphere the masses will be ready to rise up. It is a classic blueprint used by those who have already succeeded in decolonizing most of Africa and Asia. In a prosperous and well-organized society, the chances of the majority of people responding to such a group as anything but a bunch of romantic murderers are remote. But Northern Ireland can hardly be classified as a prosperous or well-organized society.

Down the Falls Road, and the narrow streets that feed it at sharp right angles, I read the slogans, a community's Dulux manifesto. 'Smash H-Block', 'IRA welcome here', 'INLA Country'. The Falls Road is the main street of Catholic Belfast, and here the gable ends were festooned with paintings that celebrated the dead hunger strikers, the first and most popular of them being Bobby Sands. Corrugated iron appeared to be fashionable in these parts, for blocking up windows, roofing ailing properties, or temporary fencing that, having been erected ten years ago, is now permanent. At the end of the streets some teenagers lit bonfires around which urchins and dogs played together in the gloom. Everything was either concrete or brick or iron; hard, definite and chillingly cold. The colours all spoke with the same dull voice, a splash of red or blue appearing as a cruel mistake. Wastelands had become playgrounds, although the streets were relatively safe as most of them had been sealed off with huge iron spikes and concrete blocks. Through the front doors of the derelict houses, the night sky was speckled with stars. The shattered pubs were open for business, but there were men at the door to check your face and religion. A common inter-factional practice involves the hurling of bombs from speeding cars through pub windows. There is hardly a pub left that has not abandoned the age-old custom of drawing the curtains at night. There are no longer any windows to draw them across.

The older people seemed pleased to see a casual stranger in the area. They sometimes smiled as if grateful, or simply nodded a greeting. The younger ones, the trainee martyrs bred on the 'Troubles', seemed enveloped in the bigotry of their birth. 'You black bastard, fuck off!' Their lives have revolved around prejudice and the application of reductive labels to all those who come from, or exist outside their own religious and political sphere. It was getting darker and many of the lamp-posts held no bulbs. The car lights began to blind and dazzle, and the slack puddles, evidence of the afternoon's rain, caught the light to give the Falls Road a momentary touch of glamour. Up above, a helicopter rattled away reminding me that Catholic Belfast can be totally isolated in a khaki flash. Out of the dark, away to my right, came the roar of a pneumatic drill. The hospital could have doubled as a prison surrounded with electric fences, surveillance cameras, buzzers and alarms. Nearby is the saddest sight, a house for sale on the Falls Road. Across the road the social centre and the fortified entrance to the snooker hall were illuminated by heavy searchlights. This whole area has become a geographical region of determination. I found it very difficult to believe that I was in Britain. It seemed so logically to be a part of Ireland, or somewhere foreign. Which is what Ireland is, foreign, a phone call from Belfast to Dublin is an international call, the crackling on the line confirming the fact. It seemed so tragically absurd.

The next day I drove south through thin mist and rain towards Ireland. I passed countless Union Jacks that flew outside schools and hung from public buildings. The police stations were armour-clad, like large pillboxes. I was happy to be leaving. Crossing the border into the Irish Republic provoked a barrage of rudely fired questions. 'Why were you in Northern Ireland?' 'Who did you go and see?' 'Can I see your driving licence?' 'Where are you off to now?' 'And then back to London?' 'What's in your boot?' 'Open it!' The soldiers crouched as though ready to shoot. As the Mozambiquan freedom fighters used to say: 'A luta continua.' The struggle goes on.

> 'I can quite understand that,' he said calmly. 'An Irishman must think like that, I daresay. We feel in England that we have treated you rather unfairly. It seems history is to blame.'
> Haines, an Englishman, in James Joyce's *Ulysses*

> The system did not presume an Irish Catholic to exist except for the purpose of punishment.
> British Chancellor of the Exchequer, 1704

Ireland is poor. The world recession, plus the dearth of industrial jobs and a baby boom, has left the country with an unemployment rate of nearly 20 per cent, and a huge foreign debt. The Irish Republic has the lowest standard of living of any of the fourteen democracies of northern Europe. One million of her 3.5 million people are either wholly or partly dependent on social welfare, and nearly half of the country's population is under twenty-five. She has traditionally depended upon migration in order that she might limp from one generation to the next, and even as late as the 1950s over a million Irish left for England, Australia, Canada, and the United States. They sent back food parcels, money and clothes to help. Some still do.

Ireland is a country of massive contradictions. A country legendary for the gregariousness of its people and their gentle disposition, yet it is inextricably involved in the continuing struggle of the IRA violently to expel the British from Ulster. It has an outstanding literary tradition, Dublin being the only city in the world to produce three Nobel laureates in literature – Yeats, Shaw, and Beckett – yet much of the country is under-educated and in some parts illiterate. However, what has always fascinated me about the Irish relates not so much to the contradictions inherent in Irish society, but more specifically to the role of Ireland in the colonization and exploitation of Africa. This was achieved by the two-pronged attack of Bible and sword. While the rest of Europe used the sword, it was the Irish who were principally responsible, particularly in this century, for supplying the Bible.

A friend of mine, an Irishman, showed me a letter he had received from an aunt, a sister in a Nigerian mission where she has spent the greater part of her life. A section of it reads as follows.

I picked up a book by a Nigerian writer, probably his doctoral thesis, and there found a challenge to all I held dear. He blamed the missionaries for bringing in a divided Christianity – different sects, and for passing this divison on to Nigerians, and using the school system to do so. Bishop Brosnahan, our own founder, had based his whole mission thrust on the schools. This contradicted the older approach used by French missionaries, of the Christian village. He knew from the Ireland of his youth that an educated Christianity is a liberating force enabling people to take their destiny in their own hands. That the people thus liberated would one day take up their pens and criticize the whole approach, is, after all, only part of the risk of calling people to life – a sign that they are alive, and a healthy thing too.

I decided to go to Dublin and seek out the pioneer missionary. On a dreary late October afternoon I found Archbishop Brosnahan at the Holy Ghost Fathers' Missionary College. The old college was grand and impressive, the landscaped grounds narrowly avoiding the vulgarity of being regal. It seemed more a place of retirement and contemplation than a hotbed of purposeful zeal. Perhaps it never was. When the Archbishop appeared I could see that he must have been tall in his youth, but now his body was slightly stooped, his gait more a shuffle than a walk. His hair had long since thinned, and as he offered his hand I noticed the blue rivulets of age. He gave me the immediate impression of a kind, good man, who was still sharp in his mind despite the fragility of his body. We sat facing each other in comfortably padded armchairs and waited silently for another retired missionary to bring in tea. The room was aesthetically bare, the décor off-white, peeling, revealing grey. The only other piece of furniture was a half-sized pool table. As I teetered on the brink of asking about this, the tea arrived carried by a missionary who looked about sixty-five. If my guess was correct, Archbishop Brosnahan must have been at least eighty. I remembered Seamus Heaney's poem, 'Station Island', the part where back in his home village the narrator confronts an old friend who tries to explain his reactions on arriving in Africa as a young missionary.

> 'The rain forest', he said,
> 'you've never seen the like of it. I lasted
> only a couple of years. Bare-breasted
> women and rat-ribbed men. Everything wasted.
> I rotted like a pear. I sweated masses . . .'

I wondered if Archbishop Brosnahan had rotted like a pear or sweated masses. Our conversation began:

CP: What is the role of the missionary?
Archbishop: To plant the church.
CP: I see. (*Pause*) Where and when did you arrive in Africa?
Archbishop: I arrived first in Sierra Leone, I think it was. Because it had a good natural harbour. That was back in 1930. I went eventually to Nigeria and set up bush schools, having taken the vow of poverty.
CP: How did the Nigerians react to you?
Archbishop: They weren't Nigerians. They were Ibo, Yoruba, and all the different tribes. I travelled by foot and contact and trust was slow. We had to take a good look at each other, if you see what I mean.
CP: And what did you see?
Archbishop: Black fellers, just like you.
CP: Just like me?
Archbishop: Some skinnier, some taller, some stouter in the girth, you know. First, I had to give them the faith, then came education.
CP: Were there many Irish missionaries at that time?
Archbishop: Lots. Many different Irish orders all over Africa. The second largest seminary in the whole world is in Nigeria. Did you know that, eh?
CP: No.
Archbishop: I know you didn't. I'll tell you something else you didn't know. When the Holy Ghost Fathers began to decline in numbers the Ibo Order, the 'Sons of the Soil', took over and they went into East Africa to try and educate the Kikuyu. They're still trying. When I first arrived there was nothing. Today in Nigeria there are fifteen universities and five medical schools. There are twelve or fourteen cardinals, and the Archbishop of Dublin himself is recommended to the Pope by a black man. And did you know that when the Pope was shot it was a black Cardinal who took his place at Lourdes?

79

CP: I didn't know that. But what of the state of modern Africa with its famine and political strife?

Archbishop: Rome wasn't built in a day. And don't forget that in seventeenth-century Europe there was a Thirty Years War. Thirty years, mind you. There's never been anything like that in Africa. (*Pause*) Do you believe in God?

CP: Pardon?

Archbishop: Are you a believer?

CP: I don't think so.

Archbishop: I baptized a dying woman out there. I asked her if she believed in God. She said, 'Did I make myself?' (*Laughs*) Now you didn't happen to make yourself, did you?

CP: (*Laughs*) No, I don't think so.

Archbishop: It's good that young men should be doing such a lot of thinking. You know the problem with the Muhammadans [Muslims] is that they did not take on the education that came with the spread of Christianity. They were left behind, and now they're trying to get into the world too quickly with their wealth.

CP: I'm not a Muslim.

Archbishop: I know you're not a Muhammadan. There was an Anglican priest in Nigeria who dressed up like them and went on the Haj to Mecca. He came back and told us it was all a load of old rubbish.

CP: But like the Muslims, the Africans had their own gods and practices when you arrived?

Archbishop: Ah, but they knew their god was not quite right. They believed in native sacrifices and evil spirits and the like.

CP: So you found conversion easy?

Archbishop: Anything but easy. It was hard work, you know. But 'God' was already in their language. We taught them the trades of carpentry, brick-laying and other such things. Eventually we, the educators, provided the basis for the African liberation movement.

CP: Yes, Mugabe was a mission-boy.

Archbishop: And Nkrumah and a lot of those brilliant fellers. The colonial Government would never educate them in this way. God is a liberating force. When a man is baptized he becomes a new creation. So Paul was a rogue, but 'Faith, Hope and Charity' were subsequently infused into his soul.

CP: Did the independence of Nigeria in 1960 change your role?

Archbishop: Well, I was already back here, but the Government invited me to attend. And one of my old boys met me at the airport and gave me a Mercedes and a driver, to get about in. His wife had a Volvo. They lived in a two-storey house, with carpets and air-conditioning. He was a lawyer who had trained in America, or England maybe, and used his education to better himself.

CP: But isn't the legacy of independence a little sad? Modern-day Nigeria is ripped asunder by coup and counter-coup.

Archbishop: You have to be good at building up the economics of the country, not just your own economics. Marx was smart, but a trifle short-sighted. He was a German Jew who had no faith or remembered religion otherwise he'd have become a famous feller. Money ruins these fellers' heads – enough is as good as a forest. Lorries that should be carrying food are carrying arms.

CP: You think they should educate, not agitate?

Archbishop: Of course, don't you? And there's plenty of missions out there helping them to educate. And they're not looking for the OBE.

CP: Do you speak any African languages?

Archbishop: Ibo. And yourself? You don't have any other language in the West Indies, do you?

CP: French, Spanish and Dutch, depending on which island you happen to be on.

Archbishop: I thought so. (*Pause*) I learned Ibo, but I preached in English. It's better for them. Allows them to go abroad for more study. (*Pause*) It was chaos. Like England before the monks made angels out of Angles. (*Laughs*) In one generation Africa has moved from leprosy, no electric lights in the bush, no schools, no water for six miles, no radio, tribal isolation, straight into the twentieth century. You can't be isolated in today's world for it's all on the six o'clock news.

CP: I suppose so.

Archbishop: Truth is the real dynamite. Being equal in the eyes of God sets you free in yourself. Then you can demand freedom for your people.

I realized that the Archbishop was tiring so I thanked him and stood up. 'Do you know where you are?' he asked. Many answers to this question raced around my brain, but I said nothing. He went on. 'Kimmage Manor. Where the woman who named Nigeria, Flora Shaw, was born.' He paused, then rolled the words around his mouth, as though savouring a good wine. 'Niger-area. Nigeria.' He led the way to the door. 'She was born here.' I was saddened to leave the Archbishop's company.

That evening I passed a gaunt young woman squatting up against a wall on O'Connell Street. 'Twenty pence for my child, mister.' Her voice was lyrical. I had no change so I walked on. She shouted after me, 'Hey mister, you're a nigger!'

A German interlude

Yet I never liked Germany. It was a country too highly organized for my temperament. I felt something American about it, but without the dynamic confusion of America.
                                    Claude McKay, *Banjo*, 1929

Munich sustained very little damage during the Second World War. Its grand buildings and monuments are a reminder of an earlier, more imperial age. Grafted on to old Munich are the new subways, precincts, and sky-scrapers of a modern and futuristic city. It is the city most Germans would like to live in. After eighteen hours I wanted to escape. The cold Germanic faces snapped round in the street to look at me. They gazed as though I had just committed an awful crime, or was about to cannibalize a small child. I began to stare back and conduct imaginary arguments. 'My skin was not burned in Europe,' I murmured silently. On the second morning I came down for breakfast and sat at a table next to a woman of about sixty. She looked at me, but said nothing. Having finished her breakfast, she pushed her plate noisily across the table and the waitress appeared. 'The *Schwarze*,' said the woman, making no attempt to lower her voice. 'He is an Englishman?' The red-faced girl said, '*Ja*.' The old woman turned to me. 'Good morning,' she said, with the chilling deliberation of a spinster-murderer. She left the breakfast room. I left Munich.

It was early November, the month that depresses me most. Four to five months of winter lay ahead as the steel cold air of Europe started to chafe my skin. Faceless eyes peered out above scarves wrapped tightly over mouths and noses, and everybody appeared suspicious as they hurried from car to shop, bus to home, shop to car. The season increased feelings of isolation and loneliness. The trees began to bow for a season and a half. In the morning half-light the tops of the big buildings were lost in a vapid roof of mist. At 11 a.m. car lights were already on.

In Frankfurt I saw more black people in half an hour than I had during five days in Munich. Most of them were American servicemen. In my hotel room the television was already tuned to the American Forces Network (AFN). On the day Indira Gandhi was assassinated the AFN news opened with a story about how well the 'super greenback' was doing against the German mark. I tried the radio and found myself listening to live coverage of an NFL American football match. When that finished I tuned into live coverage of the second half of an English soccer game on the British Forces station (BFBS). A quick spin of the dial introduced me to the Moroccan and Turkish stations. The *Wirtschaftswunder* (economic miracle) that rebuilt the nation after the last war, and produced the affluence of modern-day Germany, was due in part to the importation of immigrant labour, *Gastarbeiter* (guest-workers).

German *Gastarbeiter* have no civil rights and are liable to be deported if arrested. They have no vote and are ineligible for social security; in other words they do not officially exist. Many have to pay a German 'front' man to 'own' their video shops, restaurants, or printing works, as they are not allowed to own businesses. In order to become a German national they must have eight years' residency, no police record, pay over 3,000 marks, and pass a language examination. Unlike the British or the French, the Germans cannot co-opt their minorities by identifying and patronizing 'community leaders', as to do so would be to admit the permanence of the *Gastarbeiter* presence. Immigrants form 22 per cent of Frankfurt's population, but because they have no vote politicians are able to ignore them. In 1982 a group of fifteen professors at Heidelberg University signed a manifesto protesting against the 'dilution of the German nation through millions of foreigners and their families, the foreignization of our language, our culture and our heritage.' As George Santayana said, 'Those who cannot remember the past are doomed to repeat it'. Again it was time to leave.

There is always some poor mug hauled off the train at the West German border town of Büchen. Not everybody knows that to reach West Berlin you have to cross East Germany, which means having to produce all kinds of paperwork. The passport check often leads to the driving licence check, and on to the credit card and banker's card check. Any document that has your name clearly marked on it helps to lighten the 'Iron Curtain' bureaucracy. At Schwanheide, the first stop inside East Germany, an 'army' boarded the train, complete with dogs and unholstered guns. Guards with machine guns stood on the platform, and behind them hung huge flags of the German Democratic Republic (DDR). The 'Iron Curtain', a mile or so of no man's land, is little more than a stubble field full of trenches, slack water, and floodlights, lined with barbed-wire fences. I noticed that the East Germans love saluting – each other, passengers, and thin air. When they eventually finished with my papers and passport, I walked towards the bathroom. Some fifty yards down the corridor a roaming policeman sent me back to get my passport, then saluted.

The Hamburg–West Berlin line seems to cut through one sprawling wood, the monotony broken only by clearings of patchy fields, and old and dirty broken-down stations. Naturally the trains do not stop. As they speed through the stations the East German ticket collectors and railway officials stand to attention. To the side of the stations the small car parks appeared to be cluttered with Russian-made Lada cars, painted unusually bleak colours. By the time the train arrived in West Berlin the sight of bright colours almost blinded me. It was like changing reels from a black and white pre-Second World War movie to the Cinemascope and Technicolor of the 1950s. There was a new excitement, a Walt

Disney atmosphere on entering West Berlin.

East German television seemed just to have discovered how to zoom in and out of a shot. I sat in my West Berlin hotel watching a made-for-televison film on one of the East German channels. Every shot seemed to make use of a zoom lens. Fresh stock from the Soviet Union? And there was an unhealthily casual obsession with sex. The off-the-shoulder dresses and bikinis were gratuitous. The sharing of a post-coital cigarette, and the careful stubbing out of the butt-end into a can of 7-Up held obvious significance. As did the club and disco scenes. I thought disco died in the 1970s, but then there's no reason why the East Germans should be aware of this. I turned on the radio where the AFN female 'Jock' tried to introduce me to the idea that 'everything was cool', and we should all 'hang out for a minute, mellow back and party', as though we were at some West Coast beach party. It was snowing outside. Back to the television, and *DDR in Cuba*.

This was a documentary brimming with fraternal smiles and flag-waving, embarrassed East Germans singing salsa and swinging with the people under swaying palm trees. Then came the official planting of the tree ceremony, followed by the tying of the red Cuban scarves on blue DDR shirts. The comrades exchanged 'revolutionary' gifts. Busts of leaders, gold-leaf bound manifestos, and then a cameraman pulled a soft to hard focus on a Cuban youth toting a Kalashnikov machine-gun. The horror of this programme resided in its total lack of spontaneity. Despite the heat of the Caribbean and the irresistible rhythms of the music, both the East Germans and the Cubans managed to produce passable imitations of waxwork models. The East German cameraman contrived to shoot a carnival without any camera-shake, and nobody broke sweat. It was a clean, understated presentation of an unrecognizable Caribbean.

Out in the neon-lit streets of West Berlin, I made my way across to the Kreutzburg area of the city. It is less euphemistically known as the Turkish ghetto. There were Turkish posters on the walls, Turkish cafés, gambling joints, Turkish restaurants, and more Turkish spoken on these streets than German. Most of Germany's 1.5 million Turks live in West Berlin, but only students, poor immigrants from other countries, or Germans too poor or too stubborn to move, mix with the Turks in Kreutzburg. At the Ankara Café, the Turkish coffee was so thick I could practically stand the spoon up in it, but it provided a welcome respite from the weather. I felt quite comfortable in Kreutzburg as I ordered another stiff coffee and a beer. I passed the afternoon staring out of the window wondering if the back streets of Istanbul looked like this. I found enough material before my eyes to feed my imagination.

West Berlin is an eclectic city, its population either very young or very old with few in between. The aged remain because this divided city – the Wall being its most famous monument – encompasses both their past and their present. They are of West Germany, but geographically not of it; marooned in the heart of East Germany they have to come to terms with the fact that they are not of that country either. For the young, West Berlin offers escape from conscription, residency here allows them to avoid the duties of fifteen months' military service. The two generations of German West Berliners clash, the punk hair, striped trousers, ripped T-shirts and loud *Deutschewelle* (German punk music) of the young, is at crude odds with the discreet lifestyle of the older German population.

The Wall was constructed in 1961 and has split friends, families, parks and boulevards, injecting a peculiarly paranoid energy into the bloodstream of West Berlin. Between 1949 and 1961 nearly 3 million East Germans fled to the West via Berlin. The construction of the Wall completed the final section of the Iron Curtain and reduced West Berlin to island status. From the air the tragedy of her isolation is clear, as she appears to be little more than a badly drawn circle in the middle of an otherwise bleak landscape. Were global confrontation to ensue, West Berlin would last ten minutes.

West Berliners already seem to have learned to live as though there might be no tomorrow.

The Western side of the Wall is covered in graffiti, much like the New York subway. The Eastern side is antiseptically clean. I rode the S-Bahn to the Friedrichstrasse station where I passed through customs and into East Germany. The passport man laughed when I said I was not from Africa or Cuba. Britain seemed so unlikely, as did the fact that I already had a visa and was intending to stay in East Germany for more than the usual one day. The buildings in East Berlin, particularly the ugly apartment blocks, were more like monuments than functional offices or homes. My hotel, on the other hand, was a five-star concrete and glass tribute to Western capitalism. So much so that they refused to accept East German marks. Hotel and restaurant bills were payable only in Western currency, preferably the US dollar.

In East Berlin I sensed that being from the West was at least as important, in the eyes of the populace, as the fact that I was black. I had the ability to escape – something many of them desired but might never achieve. Each year East Germany 'sells' about 25,000 émigrés to the West, the price being around £15,000 per person, supposedly compensation for their schooling and associated education. But for every one who manages to leave, there are many more who would like to follow. In the streets of East Berlin I saw a few black people, usually students, but my casually nodded greetings were often rebuffed. It hurt, and after three days in East Berlin I was beginning to feel very detached from the West. That the stares of hostility were motivated as much by envy as by racial antagonism did little to ease my discomfort. I tried to imagine how the East Germans might be feeling. After all, what did I know about having to queue three hours for a train ticket, or buying bruised and already decaying fruit on the black market? How could I imagine what it was like to be placed on a waiting list for three years before being given the privilege of being able to purchase a dull and uncomfortable Lada or Württemburg that rattled even when brand new?

Two East German soldiers, clad in heavy winter coats goose-stepped outside the eternal flame to those who died in the struggle against Fascism. A hundred yards down the wide and imperial boulevard was the Museum for German History (*für Deutsche Geschichte*). I went in to escape the cold. Germanic history from medieval times to 1945 was contained in a small lobby. Material dating from 1945 to the founding of the DDR in 1949 was lodged in two medium-sized rooms. East German history from 1949 to the present filled the rest of this huge and architecturally impressive museum. Only a country with a profound identity crisis could pervert history to such an extent. But, of course, East Germany and her people do have a troubled and contradictory sense of self, for they share a history, a language, and a culture with the people in West Germany whom they are supposed to denounce as capitalist lackeys, although they are, both literally and metaphorically, one family. Under the West German constitution East Germans are automatically entitled to West German citizenship, though this has little meaning as they cannot use their passports to travel to the West without Eastern European exit visas.

Dusk in East Berlin is the cruellest time. Over the Wall tower the cranes of development in West Berlin. The neon lights glow against the dark sky, suggesting a circus that East Germans are not allowed to attend. I watched many East Berliners on their evening stroll who, when they came to a suitable vantage point, would simply stop and gaze over the Wall. This unsubtle proximity of the West is an unnecessary reminder of its divorce from the East. These people seemed unable to accept the division of their country as a justifiable price for the Nazi atrocities and their subsequent defeat. The separation of the country into two very distinct sociopolitical groupings was meant to ensure that Germany, the initiator of three major wars in less than seventy years, would never again be an independent military power capable of flexing its muscle. Forty years on, the almost nostalgic evening stroll that many East Berliners take, showed that the permanence of the East–West divide had yet to penetrate through to the German soul.

I travelled on to the south of the country, to Leipzig, where I finally found a copy of an English newspaper. It was the *Morning Star*, two weeks out of date. The queues in front of the shops were impossibly long. Inside there were few items for sale. The guards on the doors were presumably there to dispel any foolish notions of queue jumping or rioting. In the boutiques the fashions were sadly out of date, flared trousers being the only option. Western goods, including better quality soap, jeans, and alkaline batteries, were only available in the official foreign currency shops located in the large hotels. To watch a woman queue for twenty minutes in one of these shops to buy a tin of Nivea hand cream and a frozen pizza angered me.

I planned to spend two or three days in Dresden, but I left after twenty-four hours. It was snowing quite heavily, and the lengths of the queues had not shortened, nor had the general atmosphere of gloom abated. Dresden is not a popular city in which to live. Set in a valley, it is the only major city in East Germany that cannot pick up West German television. East Germans refer to it as the City of the Unknowing, but the Government is planning to run a cable into Dresden with West German television in order to attract skilled engineers and the best industrialists to accept postings here.

The scene on the Dresden-Neustadt station platform reminded me of a bygone age I had seen only in films or imagined in novels. It must have been in a place like this that Anna Karenina threw herself under the train. It was a sooty black Gothic monster of a station with huge arches, massive pillars, and grimy windows, some of which were broken so the stars shone through. The birds sheltered in the roof or swooped and spun around in crazy circles, trying to keep warm as the snow fell once again. As the diesel trains lurched into the station, steam rushed from their coal-fired heaters. East German and Polish military personnel, mainly teenagers, hugged their girlfriends, stamped their feet and waited.

Solitary businessmen sported Russian hats and drew deeply on cigarettes, as if this would help their circulation. They breathed out small clouds of steam, which suggested the cigarettes were heating them up. The announcements over the Tannoy were frequent, lengthy, but seldom produced any response from passengers. I could not understand what was being said; others seemed not to care. The atmosphere was bleak, haunting, and strangely beautiful.

How much more of this will we take?

Now I am homeless – a just punishment. But perhaps I was born so that the 'Eternal Slaves' might speak through my lips. Why should I spare myself? Should I renounce what is probably the sole duty of a poet only in order to make sure that my verse would be printed in an anthology edited by the State Publishing House?

Czeslaw Milosz

Mayakovsky . . . stepped on the throat of his own song.
Tadeusz Borowski, born 1922, committed suicide 1951

On the train journey to Warsaw I met an old Polish man who informed me that he had learnt his extremely rudimentary English from American movies. For some reason he assumed that I was from Senegal. I said Grenada, having decided that this might be the only Caribbean island, Cuba apart, that he would know. Months of travelling had taught that to say Britain only caused confusion. I also nurtured hopes that my Grenadian nationality might elicit Polish sympathy in the shape of an odd vodka or two, if the 1983 American invasion of the island was still fresh in people's minds. It was, but sympathy was the last thing that it elicited. To my new friend the American invasion was a 'liberation' we Grenadians should be grateful for. He then proceeded to run through the cast list of *Gone With the Wind*. There followed examples of his idiomatic grasp of English. 'Hi there, buddy!' 'What the hell is going on?' I gave him my cigars in a desperate attempt to quieten him. When we reached Warsaw he showed me where to get a legitimate taxi and avoid being hustled by the gypsy cabs. We shook hands, he turned and swaggered away with a cigar poking jauntily out of the corner of his mouth. I imagined that he now thought of himself as a compact John Wayne. 'Get the hell out of my way, I'm coming through.'

The queue for taxis was long and seemingly reluctant to move. Behind me two smartly attired young men joined the line. They held on tightly to their new attaché cases, as though guarding vital papers. I did a double take, but neither of them caught my eyes. 'Hi, are you from Africa?' I received a quick nod from the taller of the two men. 'Nigeria?' I asked. 'Yes,' said the same man. 'Studying?' Another nod. 'But you live in Warsaw?' Yet another nod, then silence. I gave up.

When I reached my hotel I found that I had been expected the previous day. I was banished to the bar-restaurant until a room was prepared for me. While there I decided to take breakfast. The girl who served me had severely laddered tights, and I turned away embarrassed that I had noticed. I stared out of the window. The swimming pool was iced over. On the chair next to me lay a discarded Polish newspaper. I picked it up, and after a few minutes' perusal came to the conclusion that the letters W, Z, Y, S and U appeared to be the most popular in the Polish alphabet. An average name could be Wczyln Ozwecuesz, or Wis for short. The waiter sidled over and interrupted my daydreaming. He surreptitiously pressed £80-worth of zlotys upon me and suggested that in return I part with a £20-note. It seemed reasonable. Then he began to draw a pencil line through about one-third of the menu. 'Shortages, you understand.' I was beginning to as I quickly pocketed the zlotys.

'Peter' thought I was a painter. I had written to him from London, announcing myself both grandly and vaguely as 'an artist' who would like to visit him when in Warsaw. We met in a student café near the Old Town. Thirty-five years of age, tall, handsome, and married with a ten-year-old son, Peter had published three volumes of poetry that had sold over 20,000 copies each. For the last nine years he had been an editor of a journal that translates the work of English writers into

Polish. He had recently translated and edited a volume of poetry by contemporary British poets, and had been fortunate enough to have extended to him the rare privilege of being allowed to take up a summer lectureship in Lincoln, Nebraska. After some initial hedging, I admitted to being a little concerned as to how the Polish authorities might receive me, were my letter to go astray and my occupation became known. He laughed, and we talked openly.

Peter regarded Poland as a part of the Third World. Despite having been introduced to his students by the American professor in Nebraska as 'a red', he felt there were benefits in being a victim of American imperialism that those in the Eastern bloc could only dream about. 'The mind is free,' said Peter. 'Do you know what a censor is? Do you know what it is to find yourself subconsciously censoring your own work?' In Poland, between the delivery of a manuscript to a publisher and its appearance as a book in print, there is a four-year gap. Only at the very last minute does the book go to the censor, and then your two years' work, and four years' waiting, six years in all, can be wiped out at the stroke of a red pen. Peter delivered a manuscript in 1982. He confidently expects the censor, in what is now the post-Solidarity chill, to 'question' a quarter of the volume, at which point he will have no option but to withdraw it and publish underground for the first time. This may result in him losing his job, it will almost certainly mean that he will never travel abroad again, and inevitably both he and his family will suffer. We fell silent as I tried to understand his predicament. Peter revived the conversation, insisting that I tell him of my first impressions of Poland. Much more cosmopolitan than I had expected, I said. 'In what way?' asked Peter. I had to admit that I was not yet sure.

The following day I visited the National Art Gallery. The examples of eighteenth- and nineteenth-century Polish art suggested a vibrant Poland in touch with Prague, Paris, Vienna, Madrid and London. In short, Poland seemed a fully integrated part of European culture at the height of its powers. In the Museum of the City of Warsaw the dynastic relationship between Poland and Sweden was continually stressed, as was the Second World War resistance struggle against the Nazis, in which 700,000 died in Warsaw alone. Warsaw's Jewish ghetto was the only one to organize and execute an uprising of any magnitude. I began to focus on a picture of a country that for the last 300 years had been manhandled by both Russia and Germany, but had somehow managed to retain a sense of national pride. Close to the Museum of the City of Warsaw is the university church. On the pavement outside lay a huge cross of flowers edged by burning candles, and surrounded by smaller crosses, some formed from lumps of coal. This makeshift memorial paid tribute to the murdered Solidarity priest Father Jerzy Popieluszko. On the backs of cereal packets, Poles had scrawled their messages. 'Hitler killed Polish priests. Now the communists are doing the same.' 'Where are these communists leading us? How much of this will we take?'

Back at the hotel my elderly chambermaid asked if she could listen to my Sony Walkman. The incantatory rhythms of Bob Marley and the Wailers shocked her more than the slick Japanese technology. 'I earn 7,000 zlotys a month,' she announced. 'A doctor earns 12,000 zlotys a month.' My mental arithmetic was not good enough to convert this into sterling, but when she pressed on with the information that an airline ticket to Montreal costs 120,000 zlotys, and a sewing machine 50,000 zlotys, I began to understand her point. 'This Government is crazy,' she insisted. 'Crazy, crazy, crazy.' She moved to leave my room, then suddenly stopped and turned around. 'You are Catholic?' she asked. She made the sign of the cross with her forefingers, but gave me no time to answer. 'In Poland, we are four in five Catholic. Five seminaries.' She spread her hand and counted them off. 'One, two, three, four, five. And a Pope.'

I decided to fly south to Katowice, but my journey began badly and continued in the same vein. On the way to Warsaw airport the taxi driver refused to turn on his meter. He wanted payment in Western currency. 'You come here, live good, eat and drink cheap, fuck our women, and you deny me $5.' Frightened of missing my plane, 'For Christ's sake just drive!' seemed the only reasonable retort. 'You make me fucking sick,' he said, as the car swung out into the traffic. We passed the rest of the journey in a surly and silent truce. At the airport I found the body search for an internal flight somewhat excessive. The customs men were armed with revolvers and knives. They confiscated a miniature bottle of vodka, informing me that it could be used as a weapon. Then, as an afterthought, they asked me if I wanted to drink it. I gave it to them as a present. In the drab and uncomfortable waiting room, I struck up a conversation with an Egyptian engineer who had been working in Gdansk for six months. He hated it. No food, no life, no clubs, no women. 'They are', he said, 'a complex, arrogant, and unhelpful people, without the necessary humility to make their situation any better.' I marvelled more at the man's English than his insight. The in-flight hospitality consisted of a boiled sweet. I took two. The plane was almost empty, apart from the two armed guards who strolled the length of the central aisle, rifles in port position.

Katowice airport was conveniently located twenty-five miles from the town. My new taxi driver, Janusz, was a tall, silvery-haired man of fifty-three, with gold spectacle frames. He was an ex-agricultural pilot who had travelled most of Europe. He wanted to know all about my home country, Grenada. As I began to expound upon its beauties, I promised myself that in future I would suffer the puzzled frowns that come with 'St Kitts', or the looks of disbelief that accompany 'Britain'. He wanted to know why Maurice Bishop was building such a large airport, why there were Cubans on the island. He continued his monologue telling me that he had not been on a train since 1968 because they were slow and totally unreliable. Goods trains have the right of way over express trains. At present, he felt that the Poles resented tourists because of the depressed economy. Tourists were able to live 'stupidly cheaply', and he personally hated trendy Western communists who littered the street corners of Paris and London with 'red' material. In fact, he had no time for the communist way of doing things. He believed that there was 90 per cent unofficial opposition, but he was doing all right because he knew the system. That, I assumed, explained why he drove a white Fiat Mirafiori and visited his daughter in Finland every year. The interrogation resumed. What was my house in London like? Was I married? Why not? Did I like Americans? I was tired, and my answers became monosyllabic. 'Don't worry,' said Janusz, 'I'll come for you tomorrow morning.' On the wall of my hotel room were large prints of Tartar herdsmen. The room still smelt of smoke from the last occupant's cigarettes. Above the bed the white wall was stained grey with the grease from countless heads. In the hotel restaurant, I found myself staring at large, fur-hatted Russian women eating caviar. Outside, the bleak grey skyline of Poland's most industrialized city turned black as night fell. I was disorientated and exhausted.

The next day Janusz drove me the thirty-five miles to Auschwitz. If there had been an airlink from Auschwitz to London, I would have taken it and flown home. In Auschwitz-Birkenau, the largest of the 5,000 camps, 4 million people were killed, 10,000 a day. The size of the figures was beyond my comprehension. At least the Atlantic slave trade had some vestige of logic, however unpalatable. Auschwitz transcended the imagination. In a courtyard Janusz pointed to a picture of a nineteen-year-old Polish gentile who had been hanged on the orders of Rudolph Hess. The beam from which he had died was still there. In fact, unlike Dachau, all of Auschwitz is still intact, which only serves to drive the horror home further. 'My cousin,' said Janusz. 'I remember him from the underground. I was fourteen. It could have been me.' He was executed for keeping in touch with the civilian resistance outside the camp. I asked Janusz if we could leave now. As we did, we drove over the train lines that cut up to the gates of the massive death camp of

97

Birkenau. I knew that Janusz was about to tell me that this was where the 'selection' took place. I glanced at him and he said nothing. We drove back in silence.

That night I woke from a troubled sleep and sat bolt upright in bed. The loud voices of American college students had shocked me into consciousness. 'You gotta see it and take some snaps. That way you really understand it.' 'Gee, they're gonna die back home when they hear I've been to a real concentration camp.' 'I don't wanna cry, but I bet I do.' 'I know a guy who couldn't eat for two days after he went.' 'Do you think Meryl Streep's been here?' They were part of a tour group visiting the camp, and like many Americans, cultural products of the television screen. Their crude responses reminded me of the American film *Cast a Giant Shadow*, written and directd by Melville Shavelson. This purported to be a responsible analysis of how a Jewish-American Second World War veteran, played by Kirk Douglas, is persuaded to aid the Zionists in the founding of Israel. In one of the early war scenes, Kirk Douglas stands outside Dachau and points. He addresses his comment to John Wayne. 'Over there's a building full of ovens, still warm, but nobody ever baked any bread in them.' In another scene he confides to John Wayne that 'We've been knocking off a lot of guys who've been making soap out of my relatives.' Clearly the students were used to Hollywood's appropriation of the Holocaust as source material for vulgar entertainment.

I had five hours to pass in Warsaw before taking my flight to Copenhagen. At Peter's apartment I met his wife and son. He lives in a small, cramped flat which the family has long since outgrown, but the chances of being rehoused in something more commodious are at best remote, but in reality non-existent. With time running out, and our friendship secure, Peter and I began to speak quickly, the conversation only slowing when he translated a particularly difficult phrase or sentence for his wife. Perhaps, suggested Peter, Western writers should be a little more like Günter Grass and protest openly at the plight of Eastern European artists. But he would not condemn those who did not. Anyhow, he mused, there were already a sizeable number who did protest. 'But what about exile?' I asked. Could he not leave and write in the West? 'But what of my family?' he countered. His family are part-Jewish, his elderly mother still living in Lodz. 'Things are perhaps not as simple as they may appear to you. I write in Polish, I am Polish, and at the moment I live in Poland. Whatever difficulties I have I must fight to overcome them here, with my family.' We shared a farewell meal, exchanged gifts, and I left. Peter showed me the dangers of a writer's role, and that it is essential for the writer to be able to protect his right not to conform. I had learnt that in a situation in which history is distorted, the literature of a people often becomes its history, its writers the keepers of the past, present, and future. In this situation a writer can infuse a people with a sense of their own unique identity and spiritually kindle the fire of resistance. Peter's struggle was a part of the larger struggle of Solidarity to establish independent trade unions that could speak with an independent voice. And finally, I had realized that I should not underestimate my privilege in being able to retreat to the West. Colonized Poland lies between the heart of the Empire (Moscow) and the front line of East Germany. The Soviet Union cannot afford to lose Poland: Poland cannot afford to lose her writers.

In the falling snow

In the falling snow
A laughing boy holds out his palms
Until they are white.

Richard Wright

By the time I reached Oslo's Fornebu airport I was tiring
badly. I had spent the greater part of a year travelling, but I
consoled myself with the thought that at least I would not
have to endure the drudgery of a long queue at passport
control. I had treated myself to Club class, and assumed
therefore that I would disembark before most passengers.
Ahead of me were two young American businessmen. They
were swiftly processed with a smile. I stepped forward and
presented myself. With one hand resting on my unopened
passport, the customs officer fired a barrage of questions at
me. How much money did I have? Where was I going to
stay? Did I have a return ticket? Had I been to Norway
before? Was I here on business? I threw down my return
ticket and stared at her, my body barely able to contain my
rage. 'Stand to one side,' she said. I stood to one side and
watched as she dealt with each passenger in turn. There were
no questions asked of them.

When everyone had gone through, she picked up my
passport and ticket, and then left her counter. Five minutes
later she reappeared in the company of a male officer. 'How
much money do you have?' he asked. I don't know. 'How
much money is in your bank account?' Which bank account?
I asked. 'Do you have any credit cards?' Yes. He nodded as
though disappointed. 'Please wait here.' They both dis-

appeared. On their return they found me looking down at the space between my feet, afraid of what I might say if I caught their eyes. 'You can proceed now.' I did not move. 'Go on, you can proceed through customs control.' I looked up and took both my passport and my ticket from the man. The sentence began from the soles of my feet and travelled right up through my body. 'You pair of fucking ignorant bastards.' 'Come with me, sir.' I was instructed to reclaim my luggage, which were the only two pieces left on the revolving belt. In gaoler-like silence, they frogmarched me into the customs hall where I was searched. A middle-aged English woman who had witnessed the episode turned upon my escorts. 'You should be ashamed,' she said. At least it was clear to somebody else what was happening. The scene could not be dismissed as paranoia, or as a result of my having a 'chip on my shoulder'.

They ushered me into the chief's office. I stood and listened as the pair of them explained, in Norwegian, to the chief the reason for my presence. As they spoke all three of them kept glancing in my direction. Eventually, the case for the prosecution came to an end. The chief put down a sheaf of papers and came over to face me. 'You must behave like a gentleman,' he told me. 'This,' I assured him, 'is how gentlemen behave when they meet arseholes.' He asked me if I found it culturally difficult to deal with a woman customs officer. I burst out laughing. He suggested that I 'leave now'. Leave for where? 'Oslo, or wherever you will be staying.' I picked up my luggage, but had one final question for him. I asked if his staff would be treating Desmond Tutu, who was due to collect his Nobel Peace Prize in a week's time, in the same manner. 'You may leave now.'

Any ideas I had of a free and easy Scandinavia had already been destroyed. Like her neighbors Denmark and Sweden, Norway is now having to come to terms with people of different cultural backgrounds, and inevitably this is producing an unpleasant backlash. Out of a population of 4 million, Norway has 80,000 immigrants, 63,000 of whom are from Europe or the United States. This leaves 16,000 non-whites, mainly originating from Pakistan and the Middle East. The non-whites constitute only 0.35 per cent of the population, yet a recent poll in the daily newspaper *Aftenposten* showed that 87 per cent of Norwegians did not want any more immigrant workers to enter the country; 33 per cent preferred not to see immigrant workers in the street; 52 per cent wanted them to abandon their cultural traditions and adjust to Norwegian life; and 94 per cent of them said they would not welcome an immigrant into their homes.

Norwegian resentment revolves around the usual fears of immigrant hygiene, unemployment, sexual fears, and displeasure at having to finance the social welfare support system that maintains some immigrants but far more Norwegians. Unfortunately, a similar bitterness exists in both Sweden and Denmark, where acts of racist violence are becoming more commonplace. Norwegian magazines, like *Innvandrer Informasjon*, which seek to promote racial harmony by featuring articles illustrated with pictures of Africans in Scandinavian clogs, are no substitute for political will. It would appear that Ibsen's century-old observation (in *Ghosts*, 1881) of his fellow countrymen still holds true: 'It isn't just what we have inherited from our father and mother that walks in us. It is all kinds of old and obsolete beliefs. They are not alive in us; but they remain in us none the less, and we can never rid ourselves of them.'

In a way, I came to Norway to test my own sense of negritude. To see how many of 'their' ideas about me, if any, I subconsciously believed. Under a volley of stares it is only natural to want eventually to recoil and retreat. In a masochistic fashion, I was testing their hostility. True, it is possible to feel this anywhere, but in Paris or New York, in London or Geneva, there is always likely to be another black person around the corner or across the road. Strength through unity in numbers is an essential factor in maintaining a sense of sanity as a black person in Europe. But, I asked myself, what happens 300 miles inside the Arctic Circle in mid-December, with nothing but reindeer and Lapps for many miles in any direction? I knew they would stare, for it is unlikely that many of them would have ever seen a black person before. Only then would I find out how much power, if any, was stored away in the historical battery that feeds my own sense of identity.

From the beginning my 'experiment' went crucially wrong. I flew to Tromsö, a town about 200 miles inside the Arctic Circle where I hired a car. It began to snow quite heavily so I checked into a hotel, then decided to find a nightclub. The first person I met in the club was a Trinidadian woman. I had foolishly underestimated the extent of the Caribbean diaspora. She was as shocked as I was, and anxious to strike up a conversation. I soon discovered that she was thirty-one, had three boys aged nine, eleven and fourteen, whose father was a Norwegian from whom she was now separated. She had met him in San Fernando, Trinidad when he was sailing through the Caribbean. Her move to Norway had caused a permanent breach with her parents and her life here with him had recently fallen apart. She was drunk, and oblivious to the leering contempt with which other men in the club watched her. Then she remembered her children. They did not like her to go out at nights, so she urged me to speak to them on the telephone. My voice would prove that she had met a West Indian and justify her neglect.

Her phone call was brief, and she returned to confess that she was anxious to leave her children and have some fun on her own. When the eldest boy reached sixteen she would be free. 'I'm still good-looking, aren't I?' she asked. 'I still can have a life of my own, but you know, I love Tromsö more than anywhere. I hate Trinidad.' She paused. 'But I have my own life now.' I asked her what she liked about Tromsö. 'The nature,' was her reply. I began to feel for the three boys waiting at home. Like a potter's wheel that has suddenly been jammed to a halt, West Indians have been flung out into history and tried to make good wherever they have landed.

She was the saddest case I had come across. Defying every-thing that I know about the caring attitude of Caribbean women to motherhood, she was lost and ailing. As I made ready to leave the club she took my arm. Did I want to meet her children? They might be asleep if we stayed and had another drink or two, and that way I would be able to meet them in the morning. I suggested that she ask somebody else and left.

The next day I drove for hours. The snow lay thick, the landscape a chilled whitewashed canvas with no human beings, just a metal forest of rickety trees, and an odd mirror-glass lake breaking the monotony. Fifty miles north-east of Tromsö I stopped for petrol in a small town. It was mid-afternoon and pitch black. The ninety minutes of winter daylight had long since passed. Turning to face me, the woman attendant dropped the petrol pump in shock. Did she imagine that I was going to molest her? I picked up the pump and gave it back to her. She made some gesture to indicate that her hands were greasy. I smiled. From the car cassette player I heard Bob Marley singing 'Redemption Song': 'Emancipate yourself from mental slavery' did not refer to black people.

I arrived back in Oslo the day Bishop Desmond Tutu received his Nobel Peace Prize. On the television he talked about the need for moral action by the West with regard to South Africa, stating that a concerted and unified economic and political embargo was essential. He made the demand in the knowledge that the vested economic interests of the West would make such action unlikely. Norway trades openly and extensively with South Africa. Their lack of moral fortitude, and that of the rest of Western Europe, will inevitably help contribute to a bloody and protracted finale to this current chapter of South African history. Norway's presentation of a Peace Prize to Bishop Tutu seemed curious. Pontius Pilate washing his hands?

The following day I attended a 'Desmond Tutu Celebra-tion' in Oslo's 'People's Hall'. Organized by the Norwegian Trade Union movement, the festivities were attended by representatives from the church and state, the laureate and his family. Again he spoke passionately on the need for 'economic pressure' and, naturally enough, he received a standing ovation. There then followed a series of performances that included a Norwegian 'punk' band, a black American singer who delivered a barely recognizable version of Stevie Wonder's 'I Just Called To Say I Love You', and a Scandinavian poet. Just when the evening seemed lost, seven blonde-haired Swedish schoolchildren strode on to the stage and proceeded to clap hands and, without accompaniment, sing a medley of African folk songs. Bishop Tutu and his family rushed to join them on stage. The spontaneity and vigour of their performance warmed an otherwise frosty evening. In this unexpected scene, there was, at last, hope.

After the celebrations I found myself sharing a table in an Oslo late bar with a drunk Norwegian. He complained to me that his fiancée had recently 'run off' to do Third World aid work in Kenya, and was now refusing to come back. In a lilting and desperate voice, he asked me how black and white can grow to understand each other. I could only tell him the truth; in many ways, we already did but that a touch of mutual respect always helped. We shook hands on it. My ten minutes of solitary peace were soon disturbed by a drunk Eritrean 'brother', who informed me that I must not stay in Europe too long as I would just get old and be pointed out as 'an old nigger'. He suggested that I go back to where I came from. He was 'studying' in Norway. I asked him how long he had been here. 'Fourteen years,' but he was quick to explain that he had only stayed for so long because he knew how to deal with the white man. An hour later I watched as they carried him out. He was unconscious before his drunken body reached Norway's sub-zero streets.

Lenin perched up a tree

Never in my life did I feel prouder of being an African, a black, and no mistake about it. Unforgettable that first occasion upon which I was physically uplifted . . . I was the first Negro to arrive in Russia since the revolution, and perhaps I was generally regarded as an omen of good luck! Yes, that was exactly what it was. I was like a black ikon.

Claude McKay, 1922

'Ladies and Gentlemen, we advise you that as we are now flying over the Soviet Union no photography is allowed, either from the aircraft, or once we land at Moscow airport.'

I looked out of the window where there was nothing to photograph, except the wing of the aeroplane and its engine. Through the wisps of drifting cloud, I could see a snow-blotched landscape with dark cancerous shadows, presumably forests. Surely this was one of the bleakest airlanes along which to approach any capital. There were no cities to fly over, and no hills to disturb the bare landscape. The Soviet Union introduced itself as bleak, cold and expansive.

I arrived in Moscow on New Year's Day, for Soviets a much more important holiday than Christmas. I was informed that Christmas does not officially exist in the Soviet Union, but, as I was to discover, official information and what unofficially happens are often contradictory. In the airport I saw two orthodox Jews, the Star of David drawn boldly across their suitcases. They were more likely to be arriving from, than leaving for, the West. They looked as lonely as I felt. The cleaners in the huge terminal building were invariably tubby women, probably in their early forties but looking sixty. They all had their hair neatly tied up and hidden away in souvenir headwraps from the 1980 Olympics. In the coffee bar the waitresses refused to smile, sadly enforcing the popular Western media stereotype of Soviet womanhood as grim prison warders.

As I waited for the bus that would take me to my hotel, I noticed a surprisingly large number of African students checking in and out of the country with suitcases and crates, hi-fis and enough books to start up several mobile libraries. The Soviet passers-by paid them little attention and were much more occupied with the sight of a party of English students who were trying to impress each other with their pronunciation of 'Gorbachev'. One girl among them insisted upon dressing like a clown, wearing ski-pants that looked like tights, winkle-pickers, luminous green socks, and bleached and shaven hair covered only when she pulled on a Second World War pilot's leather cap. Her hand luggage, a plastic laundry bag, only increased the disbelief with which the Soviets stared at her. Among her friends was a group of teenage public schoolboys, drunkenly singing Russian folk songs in a mixture of English and Russian. Clearly they had been in the Soviet Union before, but it was difficult to tell if they were singing because they were happy to be back, or if they were lamenting what they had temporarily left behind.

The journey into Moscow took over an hour. The snow made the coach's progress difficult, but on either side of us bolder lorries passed by carrying slush and grime that would be dumped into the river. The snow-clearing machines scratched a slow and deliberate path in the inside lanes, their space-age arms shovelling up the snow then spooning it into stationary trucks. The coach ploughed on. The main streets of Moscow are twice as wide as Whitehall, and broader than any I had ever seen, but the architecture that flanked them was uncompromisingly urban. I looked in awe at the housing estates that stretched for miles, their windows looking like a million dead television sets. The scale of Moscow reminded me of a Manhattan comprehensively lacking New York's glamour. Loud, sloganizing posters marked the end of one estate and the beginning of another. My first impression was of abruptness, and an almost comical lack of grace.

At this early stage it was difficult to pass any judgements on the Soviet people. All I could see were fur hats, boots and long overcoats. A few walked, but most waited with bowed heads for the bus or tram. Once in my hotel room, I looked out of the twenty-ninth floor window. Below me the landscape was a cluttered sea of tall and characterless apartment buildings. Moving between, in and around them, were Lowry-like figures in black, shuffling their way to and from work, friends or relatives. I drew the curtains.

The next morning I went for a long walk. The Soviets seemed very sure of themselves as they pushed and shoved their way to buses, casting sideways glances at those from one of the Asiatic republics, where faces were more Chinese than European. As I soon began to discover, Moscow streets abound with Asian, Mongol, and Muslim faces. In this federation of fifteen republics, Russia is obviously the most important, and Russia's capital, Moscow, the hub of the Empire. Not the 'evil Empire' that Ronald Reagan describes, never having been there, but an Empire not altogether dissimilar to the one over which he presides. It is based upon the exportation of ideology, and an economic control of other countries that often becomes dependency. But here the comparisons ended.

Eighty per cent of Moscow is made up of self-contained flats, but there is still an acute shortage of living space. Newly married couples almost invariably have little choice but to share with their in-laws. All across the city one sees construction sites, but it is seldom apartments that are being built. Memorials, memorial parks, busts, triumphal arches, these are the popular edifices. It is as though everything in Moscow has to be invested with meaning and shared communally. This is strange to Western eyes, as is the swift Soviet glance lowered at Western feet – good shoes are difficult to obtain, and footwear immediately identifies the tourist. In the hard currency shops (Beriozkas), there is little advertising or colour. These shops are designed specifically to lure foreigners into parting with their Western money. The official price for a pair of second-rate Western jeans is £55, and this explains why wearing a pair of Levis attracts not so much a Soviet glance as a longing gaze.

On the third night, I was followed by a group of Soviet youths who claimed they wanted to practise their English. I walked on for a while, but said nothing. Then, when it became clear that they intended to follow me, I stopped and asked them where they were going. 'With you.' I discouraged them but they still followed. As it is not permitted for Soviet citizens to talk with Westerners, the slightest deviation on my part towards a policeman would have made them vanish. Unlike New York or Paris where being followed by a group of youths is a problem, there was little danger here. As I passed down into the Metro station they dispersed. Whatever the game was, I was clearly not playing it.

The Metro was clean, huge and decorative. The escalators were deep enough for me to imagine that I was entering a region of Hades. In the event of a war they will double as shelters from foreign attack. On the train I sat next to a bearded middle-aged man whose understanding smile convinced me that he must be a social worker of some kind. As the train emptied he became bolder. 'Do you have anything to give my small son?' he whispered. Handing me an enamel badge in the shape of a locomotive, he introduced himself as the 'chief director' of a transport museum. 'Some English or American money, a Western badge or pin, perhaps?' I had nothing. He smiled again, looked around, and scampered off.

A few days later I joined a group tour of English and American college students. We were briskly escorted to the Kremlin and Red Square. The tour guide, Ludmila, pointed out the main Kremlin church that had been used by Napoleon as a stable. As she did so one of the group asked her how often they voted in the Soviet Union. 'Every five years,' said the inscrutable Ludmila. Then she smiled, and walked off in the direction of a smaller Kremlin cathedral.

The Kremlin is the original Moscow, a huge walled fortress of power that extends its grip across much of the known world. I listened as I wandered. 'It's quite wonderful in Moscow,' said one of the party. 'Lashings of hot water, and all the loos flush.' 'Are we gonna see the dead guy now?' asked one of the Americans, the 'dead guy' being Lenin, whose body is waxed, preserved, and on public display. The queues are always long, but after midday Westerners who present themselves and their passports at the head of the line are ushered through ahead of Soviet citizens. You are expected to file past, hands out of pocket, bare-headed, and humble in appearance. We regrouped in Red Square, once everybody had seen the 'dead guy'. I noticed that some of our party wore metal Soviet badges, not knowing what they meant. Others discussed how much whisky and vodka they were going to buy in the Beriozka. Gorbachev had recently clamped down on drinking by closing all the bars. This had led to the new sight of Westerners staggering out of the Beriozkas laden with cases of Becks and Heineken, their American Express cards safely tucked away in back pockets. As we now prepared to go our separate ways, Ludmila asked the member of the group who had enquired about voting, 'Do you have slums in England?' Laughing, she walked off before waiting for the answer. I took a bus back to my hotel, and noticed temporary pandemonium in the street as women queued beside a makeshift stall for oranges that were newly boxed and freshly arrived from Egypt.

The only places left for Westerners to order a drink and sit down were the foreign embassies. The American embassy is an imposing building on a main Moscow street. Passports and visas are checked first by Soviet soldiers outside, once through the doors American marines scrutinize them again. Then follow the body search and the questions – routine, of course. Inside the bar it was a shock to discover it full of

'Good Old Boys' drinking Budweiser and Jack Daniels. Plastered across the walls were liquor posters, interrupted only by a darts board and a Marlboro clock. Pizza, fries, hot dogs and burgers were on 'Uncle Sam's evening menu'. The 'Washington Circle' restaurant functioned only at lunchtimes. The music, a schizophrenic mixture of country and western, rock music, and black American soul, attempted to please everybody and pleased nobody.

'After General Motors, ain't nobody making as much dough as McDonald's,' began the barman. A black American marine stood to one side. He looked askance at his fellow soldiers, most of whom looked like they would end up chewing gum and running Midwestern bars. He told me that Moscow was an awful posting with one major advantage. After your fifteen months in the capital, a soldier can choose the location of his next assignment. Like his colleagues, both black and white, the soldier appeared just to be serving out his time. It was quite likely that he would leave knowing as little about Soviet life as he did when he arrived. A couple of his black friends joined us. They talked incessantly about how crazy Finnish women were – judgements derived from some practical experience. They finished their beers with a well-practised toast. 'Yeah, man! The Iron Curtain, may she rust in peace!' As I left the embassy I noticed the large American vehicles, station wagons and Buicks parked ostentatiously in the street. Up above the building, a huge Stars-and-Stripes billowed wildly in the Moscow wind.

The following night there was a party at the British embassy club. Twenty-year-old Tim from Lewisham in South London introduced himself. He had been pickpocketed twice at the West Indian Notting Hill Carnival in the summer. 'It was a bad scene, man. Really heavy. Oh, by the way, Daddy works at the embassy, and this is Amanda, my seventeen-year-old sister who's at boarding school.' Amanda and I shook hands. 'I'm at Sussex doing economics,' continued Tim. 'We just come over in the vac. I really understand why people would want to rob me though. It's so poor in some parts of Notting Hill . . .' The party was bustling with similarly cocooned diplomatic offspring, all of whom seemed to view the Soviet Union as a dour, but tolerable '18–30' holiday resort. Young West Germans rubbed shoulders with Brazilians; Africans with Americans; French met Italians, and they all drank beer, ate crisps and peanuts, and danced to Western music in a manner which led me to think that they would probably be struck dumb with disbelief were anybody to suggest that life for the youth of the Soviet Union was in any way different from their own. As I was leaving the embassy club, I stopped and watched as a young black man, clad only in jacket, shirt and pants despite the –20 degrees Celsius temperature, shouted at the two Soviet soldiers, 'I'm from Guyana!' 'Passport! Passport!' countered the Soviet guards. His voluble protestations were falling on diplomatically deafened ears. As I passed by he played his final card. Pointing to the skin on the back of his hand, he jammed his whole arm up under the nose of one of the Soviet guards. 'This, my friend, is my passport!'

His stupidity reminded me of that displayed by his former president, the recently deceased Forbes Burnham. On a visit to Moscow in the late 1970s, Burnham had been openly impressed by the perma. nt line of citizens and tourists ready to pay tribute to the waxed body of Lenin. Arrangements had been made for Burnham to be similarly waxed, preserved, and exhibited. There was one factor he failed to take into consideration – his unpopularity. If the Caribbean could point confidently to one undoubted tyrant who had plundered his country and plunged it into social and economic crisis, then that man would be Forbes Burnham. It seemed highly improbable that his countrymen would wish to pay even short-term, let alone long-term, homage to this man. Nevertheless on his death his body was duly frozen and preparation made for it to be flown to Moscow to be treated for preservation. But a power-cut, one of the many that had plagued Guyana since the infrastructure of the society began to collapse, resulted in 'our leader' thawing out and beginning to rot. All plans of permanent display had to be abandoned.

I came across another, and considerably more sober, Guyanese man, on the campus of Patrice Lumumba University. It is a medium-sized campus peopled primarily by African and Caribbean students on scholarships to read for degrees in science or political theory, with a little propaganda accompanying each graduation certificate. As the Guyanese student pointed out, the difficulties of language and weather are far bigger problems. Even before I entered the university, I had noticed many black faces pinched with cold. In the local Beriozka the men were buying cigarettes and drink to keep themselves fired up for their studies. Out in the street an African woman pushed hard at a pram in which a small baby was wrapped up like an Eskimo. Snow fell – it already lay a foot high on the ground. I said, 'Hello' and she smiled. In the pram only the baby's closed face was visible. How would the child's mother retell the tale of her Soviet sojourn, and her struggle with six-month-long Soviet winters, once back in her native Angola or Mozambique? After all, the child would have to live for ever with the distinction of having to write Moscow, USSR, under place of birth.

In the university lobby the Soviet authorities had discreetly placed a small tropical garden, consisting of a pond and some miniature palm trees. This was presumably to help make the students feel at home. The photograph of Castro on the wall was no doubt there to remind them of why it was they were in the Soviet Union in the first place. The climate of hunger and despair in the students' homelands increased the Soviet Union's hold over their futures. Precisely because the West does not care deeply or often enough, these students are delivered into Soviet hands. It is not that the Soviets are a more altruistic people, but simply that their gesture is tangible, and as the Guyanese student admitted it provoked a reluctant gratitude towards the Soviet Union, despite 'their attitude'. He spoke about this 'attitude' in a guarded manner, unlike the black American marines at the bar of the US embassy. They openly cursed the prejudiced Russians. 'And if you don't believe me,' climaxed one black marine, 'ask some of them hymies!'

'Refusenik' was a term that I had wrongly assumed to have been created by the Western media. It is a more or less accurate translation of a Russian word which refers to those who have applied to leave the Soviet Union but have been refused permission. 'Yuri' and 'Anna', and their two children, the son in his mid-twenties and a teenage daughter, are refuseniks. For the past seven years they have been applying to leave. As practising Jews, Israel was the country to which they wished to migrate, but the number of Jews allowed to leave the Soviet Union has fallen from a record 51,000 in 1979 to less than 1000 in 1985. As Jews they are forced to carry internal passports which give their nationality as *Evrei* (Jew) and their official homeland as Israel. Once they had been classified as refuseniks their lives became a nightmare.

Yuri's and Anna's flat is somewhere enmeshed in the huge labyrinth of Moscow's never-ending housing complexes. Though comfortable it is small, and much of the furniture is in need of repair. For two professional people with grown-up children, it is clearly inadequate. Yet their hospitality, warmth of personality, and generosity with time and information, transcend the quiet despair of their predicament. After his first application to leave Yuri was beaten so badly by KGB men that he had to spend two months in hospital. He was not beaten in some back street, in a van, or in a police car, but in open daylight outside his apartment. It is entirely possible that his life was saved by an old woman who pleaded tearfully with the three KGB men who were kicking him unconscious. He only kept his job because of 'outside protest', but in a country where it is illegal and punishable by imprisonment not to have a job, he still lives with the threat of dismissal. Worse than this is the possibility that the authorities might wipe his name from the university records. Such bureaucratic vandalism means that the state could deny his scientific qualifications altogether, and he would no longer be qualified to do his job. Not surprisingly, both he and his wife felt very bitter that the West knows so little about the conditions of life in the Soviet Union.

American relatives, who were planning a trip to Europe, had written to Yuri suggesting that they meet in Paris, or, failing that, Warsaw. 'They didn't understand,' he said with exasperation, 'that we can't even go to Leningrad without proper authorization and clearance. It is good that television films such as *Sakharov* are made [he had managed to view it on a smuggled video tape], but they [the West] romanticize the situation.' Yuri stood up and paced about the small room. 'The Soviet Union is worried about her internal economic plight, and is, image-wise at least, softening her line with the Americans. But' he warned, 'it still has designs on the West. And is still full of interior repression and exterior hypocrisy. How else can you offer to sell a man [Anatoly Shcharansky] for $1½ million? We are not cattle', he said, 'to be bought and bartered with. You, of all people, must know that.'

I tried hard not to let Yuri's words prejudice me, but his story made me see the country in a different light. It was impossible to obtain most of the foreign press, and many foreign radio stations were jammed. Clearly the only way up in the society was via the party machinery, which demanded unswerving loyalty to the State. For ordinary Muscovite workers the most treasured and least aimless jobs are those in hotels, Beriozkas, anywhere that provides contact with Westerners or Western cash, for any foreign currency went far. Despite the slogans, the queues, and the exterior drabness, I tried hard to persuade myself that it would be a mistake to assume that the Soviet Union was peopled by Yuris, or those who were critical of the system. I also tried to persuade myself that it would be equally wrong to assume that only Westerners have a bright future to look forward to. But out of this maze of reasoning I now found myself in real danger of becoming the sneering capitalist, obsessed with the lack of consumer goods, ignoring the more positive aspects of the Soviet welfare and educational system. But would I really want to receive medical attention or schooling in the Soviet Union?

The rewriting of Soviet history has been perfected until it is now a fine art. Trotsky is absent from photographs, street names, and history books. A university lecturer informed me that Trotsky was a 'maverick', and that there were dozens of others just as important as Trotsky in the history of the Revolution of whom we, in the West, had never heard. At his private seminar, in a room of a large Moscow hotel, he went on to inform a group of English students that perhaps the 1917 Revolution had moved too quickly, and that in two or three generations everything would be all right. He hypothesized that the 'black market' would naturally die out as the Soviet Union began to manufacture 'desirable hi-fis at a reasonable price'. This picture evoked laughter. After talking of the need 'to let economic lungs breathe', he reminded us all that the Soviet slogan for 1986 was the catchy 'Let's make the country more economical.' Before I took my leave, I asked him about the role of Soviet writers. 'Good doctors of the society,' he said. 'They keep the pulse of the State, and we like to encourage them. There are 7,000 officially sanctioned and unionized writers in the Soviet Union. How many have you in your country?'

My final day was spent making a whirlwind tour in a fierce blizzard. At the Soviet Palace of Culture the grim ugliness of the Stalinist architecture depressed me. The brochure suggested that, 'The absolutely correct geometrical lines are the embodiment of the concept of "the aesthetics of the right angle", and its precise proportions make the building astonishingly beautiful.' The Palace of Culture was attached to a car factory that employs 125,000 people, and each day 8,000 to 9,000 people 'visit' the Palace for recreational purposes. I looked at the men vainly struggling in life drawing classes, or blowing wind instruments, and I knew that under a different system they would be in a working men's club, or playing snooker or darts, or just drinking a pint. After all, who in their right mind wants to spend three hours every evening (Monday to Friday) practising with 'the Russian song choir of the civil engineering workshop of the Likhachov motor works'? But, at the end of a long, hard day at work these people had no choice but to attend. I had seen my first forced leisure camp, and it was only one of fifteen centres in Moscow. The idea was simple: keep the people busy so they see, hear and do nothing other than what you tell them. Soviet tourist guides practise this same technique on Western visitors.

'The Exhibition of Soviet Economic Achievement' was housed in eighty exhibition halls, spread over 600 acres, and attracted 12 million visitors a year. To look at what? Sacks of wheat in the 'Agricultural Hall'; miniature models of sputniks in the 'Space Hall'; and foxes, minks, sables, and rabbits awaiting their metamorphoses into hats and collars, in the 'Furs Hall'. This kind of propaganda fair is not unique to the Soviet Union. It was the massive exhibition of Soviet Realism, attracting large crowds to one of the national museums, that repulsed me. The angular paintings, technically inept, and lacking in any heart, all paid homage to the stifled imagination. The individual in a social context, the image designed solely to feed the flag. A smiling girl behind the wheel of a tractor. A youth stripped to the waist manfully pulling a cart – doing the work of a mule. A helmeted cosmonaut waves, fulfilling his Soviet duty in space. Industrial grime and greasy labour glorified. In an inappropriately large number of these pictures the image of Lenin appears. In the background of a 'workers' meeting' scene, and earnestly taking notes, sat Vladimir Ilich. Then in the 'factory canteen scene', breaking black bread with the peasants, would be the man himself. A picture of a forest makes you think, 'Thank God'; then it strikes you that if you look too closely Lenin may appear perched up a tree.

While waiting to leave at the airport, I again noticed the African students on their way to or from Patrice Lumumba. I pondered how it was they could have become so dependent on such a system. But, then again, Europe is dependent too: Eastern Europe on the Soviet Union, Western Europe, increasingly, on America. Perhaps the surprise lies only in that Britain's or France's slide under the eagle has been much less abrupt than Poland's under the hammer and sickle. The analogy is crude, but it still did not answer my initial question. I suppose all I was really asking was 'Why don't the Africans get more help from the West? Wouldn't they prefer it instead of having to come into this hellish climate and grapple with the Russian alphabet?' But few poor countries really care where help springs from initially, East or West, as long as they get hospitals, schools, roads and bridges. The Soviets know this, and they know that to give a man knowledge (especially in the Russian tongue) places that man in their debt for ever. Politics comes after aid, but by then it is often too late. The provider may well have become the colonizer. However, watching the students I found it difficult to believe that they were in too much danger, it seeming a geographical, climatic, and linguistic nonsense to imagine that the Soviet Union might put down roots in either Africa or the Caribbean. A Russian in 30 degrees Celsius heat dancing to a drumbeat? But then again I was looking at fur-hatted Africans in −20 degrees Celsius.

The European tribe

> To be rooted is perhaps the most important and least recognized
> need of the human soul.
>
> Simone Weil

The England that I returned to after nearly a year's travelling
was caught in the tight grip of a recession. Tired of con-
tinental hotel rooms furnished with wardrobes that looked
like upended coffins, I had imagined that I would be pleased
to be back in London. But, as if I had never left, I found the
capital stimulating but not sustaining. The days were short
and dull, the weather a perpetual drizzle, the people slouched
around the streets afraid of the 'future'. Britain did not seem
that different from the rest of Europe, and I was surprised
that I had imagined it would. It appeared to me now, even
more so than before my departure, indivisible from the rest
of Europe and exclusive in its attitude toward me.

Since the Second World War Britain has had to make a
major reassessment of her position in the world. Empire
involuntarily gave way to Commonwealth, which in turn
gave way to Common Market. This reductive pattern
appears to be causing much anguish in the bosom of the
British nation, as it ushers in a new age in which Britain will
have both to collaborate and co-operate with others. This
process of reassessing her status will continue to prove painful. Involvement in discussions about a Channel tunnel, a
common European currency, and freedom of movement
across borders is a sad step down from the aloofness of just
two generations past. There are those, however, including
people in the highest Government positions, who find it

difficult to accept this state of affairs. For them it is useful to imagine that Empire still exists, in order that they may occasionally fan nationalistic pride and galvanize the nation, in war if necessary.

St Helena and her twin, Ascension Island, 700 miles to the north-west are, like Hong Kong, Gibraltar, Northern Ireland, and the Falkland Islands, examples of a post-colonial British legacy, rich white jewels in a slightly askew crown. They are a huge burden on the British taxpayer, and it has now reached the stage where, because of a series of complex Nationality Bills, some British passports have been devalued to second-class status. Northern Ireland apart, these other 'Britons' have no automatic right of entry or residence. An American passport is no more or less than its title states. Holding a British passport can, these days, mean anything. This is because Britain, the nation that once possessed the finest fleet in the world to guard her shores, can no longer afford to think of herself as an impenetrable island. Her colonial legacy has returned to haunt her, the armada she launches these days consists of White Papers from Westminster which are read with relish at the ports of Dover and Heathrow.

Britain's and Western Europe's days of imperialistic glory are history. The former slaves wander freely among the rubble of Europe's formerly all-powerful cities, while Eastern Europe appears already to have entered the new phase of Soviet imperialism. Eager to avoid the still hungry Soviet bear, the rest of Western Europe has joined Britain in cowering under the shadow of Washington's eagle. America, the Frankenstein that Europe created, has risen from the slab. An American president visiting Moscow will stop in Paris or Bonn only on his way home; a French or German president will be expected to visit Moscow by way of the White House. The young, arrogant country to which the second-rate Europeans, the crooks, the poor, the starving, the inferior minds and the misfits, escaped, then continued to behave like Europeans by slaughtering the native Indians and enslaving the blacks, is now no longer behaving in a European manner. America has conquered Europe economically, politically, and culturally. The country is populated by an upwardly mobile, iconoclastic, energied people who leave their mark on whatever they touch, and scorn any alternative cultures. I have sat in Barbados sipping 7-Up through a 'Keep America Clean' straw – a neo-colonial experience. America, with improved mass communication, is growing into a more united nation (*USA Today* is, despite the bulk of the States, a national daily).

By contrast, Europe, at this late hour, is trying to forge a new unity through trade, despite the divisions at the heart of European consciousness, as squabbling tribes stare at each other across national boundaries. Politically in a state of panic, economically no longer dominant, Europe seems now to be left with only the role of moral leader to play.

But before she can become a moral leader she must go to confession. She must not be too proud to admit that she is in the same position as much of the Third World in terms of an increasingly paranoid allegiance and dependency on one camp or the other. And she must acknowledge that the continued toleration of racism in her belly threatens to consume any chance of a positive moral initiative. She still looks askance at 'strangers' as they alone reinforce a sense of self. Ultimately, the one certainty for Europe is that she knows a 'nigger' when she sees one: she should – they were a figment of her imagination, a product of her creative mind.

Europe's absence of self-awareness seems to me directly related to a lack of a cogent sense of history. It is no coincidence that at the great European schools of learning, history is still the most respected of degrees. But history is also the prison from which Europeans often speak, and in which they would confine black people. It is a false history, an unquestioning and totally selfish one, in which whites civilize and discover and the height of sophistication is to sit in a castle with a robe of velvet and a crown dispensing order and justice. When Bokassa aped it, Europe mocked simply because she could not stand to look at herself. Such history involves superiority and inferiority, so that when the Japanese, who used to be inferior, began to find a voice technologically and economically, the Arabs oil, and the Jews a country, it left Europe with only the blacks and themselves to despise.

Britain, more than any other European country, is at present playing a very dangerous game. Riots continue to happen, perpetrated by British people. The discontented are not immigrants, as 40 per cent of the black population in Britain was born here. The attempts of politicians and the media to ignore the violence of feeling, while discussing 'integration', 'racial harmony', and 'multiculturalism', only serve to aggravate the situation. It is no surprise to find that the English language seems to hold more terms of racial abuse than nearly any other language. There is little necessity for euphemism when words such as coon, dago, paki, nigger, spade, yid, kraut, frog, and argi abound. An unwillingness to deal with change in society, and by extension that society's image of itself, characterizes modern Britain and permeates the language of all classes.

The importation of post-Second World War foreign labour was a Western European phenomenon. Britain simply had the largest pool of colonial migrants on which to draw, but countries such as France and Germany were able to exploit the poorer Europeans such as the Spanish and Portuguese, and the freely available Turks, as well as their colonies. But whether 'guest workers' or 'colonial migrants', the role of these workers was the same: to help build up the economies of a Europe ravaged by a second major war in thirty years. Foreign labour became an inextricable part of healing European economies, but it is only now, as technology makes labour increasingly obsolete, that an excuse is needed to explain the current malaise. Immigration is no longer a problem, for all Western European governments stopped the entry of workers at almost exactly the same time in 1973–4 – a compromise between the interests of capitalism and the fears of public order (Britain was a decade ahead of the rest with the 1962 Immigration Act). Europe's current 'problem' relates directly to the permanence of our presence, not our continued arrival. Our refusal now to do the decent thing and conveniently disappear is all too often served up as the 'excuse' for the sickness in Europe's soul.

Immigration follows a classic three-stage pattern. First, there is the phase of labour movement, whereby single males leave to seek out the opportunities and find a place for the family. Then comes the second phase of family reunification, which may take months but often takes years. Then, as the family settles and the children grow older, there comes the final stage of settlement as memories of the old country begin to recede and the first-generation immigrant begins to develop at twice the speed of the country that he has left behind. This virtually ensures that it will be impossible for him to return. Britain differs from Western Europe only in as much as she is further advanced in the settlement phase, having encouraged the process of mass migration at an earlier date. Settlement is the most crucial phase, for it is at this stage, particularly if the host country is experiencing economic difficulties, that the media and politicians start to promote the image of immigrants as the cause of the difficulties rather than seeing them as fellow victims. Society, taking a lead from the media and its politicians, begins to reject a whole class and marginalizes them in the job market. Inevitably this results in civil disturbance as a sophisticated second generation, who identify with Third World struggles and are keenly aware of the hypocrisies at the heart of this Europe, begins to strike back. This is exactly what is happening in Britain. The picture is only slightly complicated by the emergence of neo-Nazi groups on the political scene.

It is no longer possible for a European to dismiss Fascism as the grandiose dream of a lunatic fringe: there is good evidence that right-wing extremism is on the rise again all over Europe. Historically, Fascism has garnered its support from the lower-middle classes, those most threatened during the time of a recession who fear the working-class status to which they might return through the economic ruin of their corner shop or the closing down of the components firm where they hold a white-collar job. Fascism gives such people explanations for the situation in which they find themselves, and a way of changing their situation with 'action' not 'words'. They can become political by sidestepping the intellect and organizing society not into classes but race. This is useful, and it enables them to have a temporary empathy with people they might otherwise never meet socially.

For the working classes, Fascism bestows a sense of worth, makes them feel part of a society that is usually unwilling to grant them anything. No matter how poor you are, you are better than the Yid or the spade; you are of the 'master race'. The present economic crisis is of a proportion that capitalism has never experienced. At present there are over 20 million people unemployed in Europe, and the figures are unlikely to improve. The general hopelessness and disillusionment of Western Europe is ideal soil in which to plant Fascist ideology, with its simplistic racial equations for complex socio-economic problems.

In British schools adolescent support for the Fascist National Front has increased. Pupils know little about such parties, except that they are in favour of 'expulsion' of all 'New Commonwealth' immigrants. It will, so the logic assures, provide a quick, simple, and final solution to Britain's problems. Among the British professional classes, dealing with the problem of the 'educated' black involves co-option. This means that black people have ended up fighting for top posts in the race relations industry. They are effectively 'bought out' of the mainstream. How many of the 'equal opportunities' local authority employers are managed by blacks? How many black bank managers are there? At the time of writing there are not even any black MPs. Black people in Britain are not, like the German *Gastarbeiter* or the French Africans, living in dingy, hopeless hotels or cheap barracks, but they are often made to feel as though that is where they belong. The fact is that most white Britons do not know a black person, let alone what one might want. They dare not imagine that black people might be just like them and want economic and political power, for that would be too bitter a pill to swallow and a sign of audacious ingratitude. But until black people in Britain take economic and political power they will remain easy prey for those who would lodge them permanently in the periphery. It is only a matter of time before the power is seized – for it will not be given. Until then the tension will not slacken.

I can almost hear the objections as I write. 'You really can't be accusing intelligent, educated people of the ignorance you associate with blind bigotry?' However, the truth is that it is precisely these people that I am accusing above all. While I was still a student, somebody wrote 'Go home, nigger' on the college notice board next to my name. It must have been there for the greater part of the day before I saw it, but not a single student, tutor, nor the college porter erased the insult. When I left college I was quizzed by a social security official as to whether the girl I lived with was black or white before being offered forms for benefit. In recent years a BBC Television producer asked me what African languages I spoke, and if I spoke them when I'm with other West Indians. A leading theatre director refused to believe me when I pointed out, with reference to a play I had written on the subject, that 11 million Africans had travelled the 'middle passage'. 'Don't be bloody ridiculous,' was his reply. At a London publishing house, an editor referred to me as a 'jungle bunny'. All good 'liberals' to a person. It is neither healthy, nor desirable to spend one's whole European life aware of 'colour', and I have yet to meet a single black person who enjoys it, but the curiously warped logic of the European continually attempts to force this upon us.

The crisis of a second-generation black British community, with no viable alternative to offer in either language or religion, will deepen in direct proportion to the vigour with which Britain tries to ignore the gross inequity of opportunity, thus further aggravating socio-cultural differences by unwittingly encouraging people to waste precious energy on the cultivation of conflict, energy which should be harnessed and used in the cause of mutual understanding. I cannot write in Yoruba or Kikuyu, any more than a black youth born in Peckham or Middlesbrough can hope to feel at home in Addis Ababa or Kingston, Jamaica. His excellence, his ability is all that he has to offer British society, and any society in the world should be grateful to receive it. If he is told in many subtle and differing ways that he is nothing, he will give nothing in return. A new swimming pool opened nearby my home in London. On the first day I went there I heard a small girl's voice cry, 'Mummy, that man's dirtying the water.' What conversations and home environment had produced that statement? On hearing her mother's answer I could guess. 'Be quiet, Shelley. He's just a darkie.' As James Baldwin once remarked, it makes you wonder if you really do want to be part of a burning house.

I fear the prolonged wandering of the displaced, who inevitably become the victims of handy theories, particularly if the host country is in trouble. The resultant cultural dislocation they suffer has a longer and deeper effect than mere physical displacement. There is a danger that clichés, symbols or metaphors will be reached for, to substitute for being 'rooted'. 'Africa' is the obvious example with reference to black people in Britain. But it seems to me that black people who are trapped in a hostile and racist Europe, exiled from a politically and economically unreliable Caribbean, are beginning to gather around themselves the values of survival and resistance that have sustained them on two journeys across the Atlantic, and are now fighting for the right to be a part of the future of this continent. The legitimate response to hostile European eyes is, 'Well, you shouldn't have gone there in the first place. And if you hadn't caused so much misery and underdevelopment down there, I might not be here now.' The causes of British rioting are rooted in this look and its stern rebuke. Rioting is an international phenomenon, part of a long tradition of violent reponse to ignorant rejection.

Deprivation of itself is not enough to produce riots, and this is why simply pouring cash into inner city areas to build facilities is an act of folly. What is of paramount importance is relative deprivation, the feeling that the terms on offer are unjust. Life in a consumer society, where the virtues of mass consumption are preached repeatedly every day, on television and in print, inevitably leads to tension as people seek to gratify the needs they are conditioned to feel. Housing is bad, but no worse than fifty years ago when there was massive unemployment, no adequate benefits system – and no rioting. A sense of relative deprivation, coupled with feelings of valuelessness, and of having no investment in the society, no grip on the steering wheel of power, this is what makes people riot.

Clearly, it is now necessary for Europe, and Britain in particular, to purge herself, perform a historical striptease – in private, if a public display is too embarrassing. It is crucial for white Britons to understand that the African was the flexed muscle of the British Empire, an Empire the British never gave up. They were simply unable to hold on to it. They must also understand that no black children, when asked about their future and what they want to be when they grow up, ever answered 'underprivileged', 'a minority problem', or 'a slave'. Britons should also ask themselves just what are the 'benefits' of being white? Whites have visible economic, political, and social superiority, but underpinning all this is a powerful history which makes possible a secure sense of collective identity. In your churches, education, government systems, architecture, music, arts, you belong to a group which exports a culture to every corner of the world – you are a part of the European tribe. Brazilians, Mozambiquans, Angolans speak Portuguese; Central and Latin America, Spanish; most of Africa, America and India, English; other parts of Africa, the Far East and the Caribbean speak French or Dutch; even older Ethiopians speak Italian. Wherever you go in the world, you can carry with you the evidence of your visible achievements, and they will be universally recognized. In this way you develop your own tough identity muscles.

But history has decreed that we, black people, must dig deep for the evidence of our equally great contribution, and cling to it in the face of ignorance. That Pushkin and Dumas were black is not a statement of fact when made to a European, but the opening line of an argument the European will be happy to lose, knowing that they can be replaced ten times over with Shakespeare, Dante, Milton, Kafka, and Tolstoy. You do not ask why you can do this, nor if there may be other black achievers and achievements of which you have hitherto been ignorant. You justify your Empire, your actions, your thought with your 'civilization', forgetting that in this century, in the Congo, Belgians chopped off black hands and feet as legal punishment for under-production. As I write, your cousins in South Africa, a distant European tribe, prepare to fight for their economic future by killing black women and children in cold blood. Your eyesight is defective. Europe is blinded by her past, and does not understant the high price of her churches, art galleries, and architecture.

My presence in Europe is part of that price. I was raised in Europe, but as I walked the tiny streets of Venice, with all their self-evident beauty, I felt nothing. Unlike Othello, I am culturally of the West. I stood on the Rialto and thought how much more difficult it must have been for him, possessing a language and a past that were still present. Nothing inside me stirred to make me rejoice, 'Ours is a rich culture', or 'I'm a part of this.' I responded coldly to the aesthetics, but recognized the traditions. I could find little empathy with the cultural bravado of a Eurocentric past. Should I have made an effort I knew would never be reciprocated? Despite my education I found myself then, and still now, unable to engage with a Eurocentric and selfish history. Black people have always been present in a Europe that has chosen either not to see us, or to judge us as an insignificant minority, or as a temporary, but dismissible, mistake. I looked down at the Grand Canal and realized that our permanence in Europe no longer relied upon white European tolerance, or the liberal embrace, but made a much more radical demand. Europe must begin to restructure the tissue of lies that continues to be taught and digested at school and at home for we, black people, are an inextricable part of this small continent. And Europeans must learn to understand this for themselves, for there are among us few who are here as missionaries.